0/25/82

Breakthrough:

Women in Television

Other *Breakthrough* titles

Breakthrough:

Women in Television

By Betsy Covington Smith

Walker and Company
New York

LIBRARY OF CONGRESS CATALOGING IN PUBLICATION DATA

SMITH, BETSY COVINGTON.
  WOMEN IN TELEVISION.

  (BREAKTHROUGH)
  INCLUDES INDEX.
  1. WOMEN IN THE TELEVISION INDUSTRY — UNITED STATES —
INTERVIEWS.   I. TITLE.   II. SERIES: BREAKTHROUGH (NEW
YORK, N.Y.)
PN1992.8.W65S57   1981   791.45′092′2   80-54704
ISBN 0-8027-6420-7   AACR2

FIRST PUBLISHED IN THE UNITED STATES OF AMERICA IN 1981 BY THE
WALKER PUBLISHING COMPANY, INC.

PUBLISHED SIMULTANEOUSLY IN CANADA BY JOHN WILEY & SONS
CANADA, LIMITED, REXDALE, ONTARIO

ISBN: 0-8027-6420-7

LIBRARY OF CONGRESS CATALOG CARD NUMBER: 80-54704

PRINTED IN THE UNITED STATES OF AMERICA

10 9 8 7 6 5 4 3 2 1

For Adair, Carter, and Adam
with love

Contents

INTRODUCTION

"I believe television is going to be the test of the new world and in this new opportunity to see beyond the range of our vision we shall discover a new and unbearable disturbance of the general peace or a shining radiance in the sky. We shall stand or fall by television — of that I am quite sure."

— E.B. White, 1938

TELEVISION CAME TO AMERICA in the late 1940's, during the boom years following World War II. All of the doubts and all of the dreams that E.B. White had expressed a decade earlier accompanied its arrival.

To the dreamers, television promised a bright new world that would open up people's minds and hearts and horizons. Imagine! More people would be able to see a single televised performance of Shakespeare's *Hamlet* than all of the theatre audiences in all past history put together. The great geniuses of science would enter living rooms and explain their discoveries. The world's most gifted musicians, poets, and playwrights would bring music and art and drama to the home screen. The camera would whisk audiences off to places and events around the world, putting an end to isolation and provincialism forever. In the words of Sylvester (Pat) Weaver, one of the pioneering figures of early television, this new medium would make "the common man the uncommon man."

For every dreamer there was a doubter. Among these were the broadcasting executives themselves. American television came out of radio, with the same broadcasters who had brought sound to the nation now in charge of bringing people a combination of sound and pictures. But in the 1940's, most broadcasting executives felt that television would never amount to anything but a toy for the rich. Television sets were expensive. The technology still hadn't advanced enough to produce clear pictures on television screens. By mid-1947 receivers were being manufactured at a rate of only 160,000 a year. During this period one young man who sought the advice of Dr. Frank Stanton, president of CBS, about whether or not to go into broadcasting recalls that Dr. Stanton was enthusiastic, but that he advised the young man to stick to radio. There was never going to be much money in television, he said.

And then, very suddenly, television took off. No invention of the twentieth century, with the single exception of the automobile, changed the habits of Americans so rapidly or so permanently. It appealed to everyone, regardless of age, occupation, nationality, social status, or education. Between mid-1947 and the end of 1948, the number of TV stations increased from 10 to 127. In 1950, 7,355,000 television sets were sold, a figure that doubled the following year. By 1980, 76.3 million households (not people!) had television sets with the average set turned on six hours and twenty-six minutes each day.

Television came into my life when I was fourteen. I had grown up on radio, insatiably listening to programs similar to what later became the basic format for television programming. Then, one bright Saturday morning in the spring of 1952, two burly men arrived at our house and heaved an enormous piece of furniture containing a television screen out onto our sun porch. (There were no portable sets back then.) Out went our old 1930's floor-model radio; in its place went this giant eye that looked straight out of science fiction. The men hooked it up and pressed a button. My family and I drew closer, scarcely daring to breathe. After what seemed an interminable length of time, the dark screen brightened, and moments later a fuzzy, quivering black-and-white picture came on. I don't think I'll ever forget that moment—the idea that we were actually *seeing* something that was taking place miles and miles away. It seemed pure magic, fascinating and terrifying at the same time.

Prime-time television in the 1950's has been called "The Golden Age of Television"—and, indeed, it was frequently quite wonderful. All network programs were broadcast to the nation live from New

York. There were game shows such as "What's My Line?," celebrity-studded revues like "The Ed Sullivan Show," comedy hours such as Sid Caesar and Imogene Coca's "Your Show of Shows," situation comedy series like "The Honeymooners" and "I Love Lucy." And there was theatre—real, live theatre that each week presented full-length plays written for television. Usually these plays were filmed on a small theatrical stage. There were few scene or costume changes. The cast was given scripts to study, roles to memorize, a period of time for rehearsals. Then, on the appointed night, the company performed before the cameras exactly as it would before an audience. And the audience, which numbered in the millions, saw everything instantly, including flubbed lines.

Men ran television, there was never any question of that. Male executives made the all-important decisions about what people would see; men producers, directors, editors, cameramen, and writers created the shows; men from television sold commercial space to men from the advertising agencies; men correspondents went after the news, wrote it, and reported it to a waiting nation. In short, both on-camera and behind-the-scenes, from executive decisions to production, sales, news coverage and analysis, men were in charge of the serious side of television.

Women were the fluff. From the beginning days of television, women were always represented among the ranks of on-camera performers. They danced on TV, they sang, they did comedy routines, they served as panelists on game shows, and they acted in dramatic roles. Television entertainment, which has always been the heart of network programming and the source of its greatest profits, couldn't ignore them. Women were part of life. For every boy there had to be a girl. For every man, a wife.

By the beginning of the 1960's, American television had come of age. It had grown into a very big and very, very profitable business, one that provided advertisers with the largest audiences the world had ever known. The practice of live broadcasts ended. Film was more practical and more profitable because filmed programs could be reused and resold to advertisers. With the coming of film, the entire entertainment side of the industry moved from New York to the West Coast, the center of the film industry.

Each year brought new improvements in television technology. Viewers began getting clearer pictures on their screens. Television xii *Breakthrough:* Women in Television

sets became smaller and more manageable. The U.S. Space Program ushered in the era of satellite communications, allowing the public to see anything in the world at the moment it happened. Videotape was perfected, becoming an increasingly used production technique. Finally, as the decade drew to a close, color television with vivid, true-to-life tones began replacing the old black-and-white sets in American homes.

There was one aspect of television that did not change much during the 1960's—the role that women played within it. The men who ran things did not take women seriously and they did not expect their viewers to, either. On news programs women were the weather girls; for documentaries they were the researchers; at the executive level . . . well, there was always room for secretaries.

Av Westin, ABC's vice-president and executive producer of the national nightly news, recalls how it was back then: "If you found a woman you wanted to move along, there was, well, not really what you could call resistance, but you'd get some raised eyebrows." A former head of NBC News blamed viewers for the attitude toward women when, in 1971, he said, "Audiences are less prepared to accept news from a woman's voice than a man's."

There were, of course, a few exceptions—women whose brains, perseverance, and talent couldn't be ignored in such a talent-intensive industry. They stood out then and they stand out today. Because of them, the women who followed were more easily accepted.

In 1964 Barbara Walters rose from being an obscure writer for NBC's "Today" to being one of the on-air cohosts. Other women had preceded her on the show, including Lee Ann Meriweather, Helen O'Connell, Betsy Palmer, and Maureen O'Sullivan. But these women, though accomplished in their own fields, were not journalists. Known as the "'Today' girls," they were required to do little more than smile prettily, read commercials, and engage in mindless chatter. In contrast Barbara Walters projected intelligence, directness, and an immense talent as an interviewer. What's more, these qualities were what made her so popular with viewers. Not only was she never called a "'Today' girl," she never acted like one.

Behind the scenes a few other women were distinguishing themselves as well. In 1963 Lucy Jarvis, who had been in broadcasting since the early 1950's, made a name for herself as the producer of

NBC's dazzling documentary "The Kremlin." By the end of the sixties she had accumulated a long list of memorable documentaries. Meanwhile, over at New York's noncommercial station, channel 13, Joan Ganz Cooney was rising through the ranks. Her career culminated in 1969 as the creator and guiding spirit behind the new and educationally innovative children's series "Sesame Street."

The 1960's was a time also when a few women managed to become "first" women in the area of on-air national news. In 1964 Marlene Sanders, who later became the first woman vice-president of a network news division, was briefly an anchor for the national news at ABC. Marya McLaughlin began reporting for CBS. And, in 1968, NBC sent Liz Trotta to Vietnam, making her the first woman on television ever assigned to cover a war. When she returned to New York after her arduous six-month assignment, however, an NBC executive grinned at her and said, "You've got to admit that was a great stunt to send you there."

The men of television did not suddenly wake up one day and repent over their traditional exclusion of women from the industry. Reforms came as a direct result of the women's movement of the late 1960's. Women were fed up and ready to fight for change in courtrooms of law. In the early 1970's word was passed from one network to the next and down to their wholly owned local stations to begin hiring more women on all levels. Realizing the legal necessity of providing equal employment opportunities, the men who ran things were clearly uneasy about the existing situation. They had good reason to be nervous. In February 1977 NBC paid a $2,000,000 out-of-court settlement as a result of a sex discrimination suit that had been brought on behalf of all its women employees.

Slowly at first and then in increasing numbers, women in the early 1970's began moving into areas of television that had once been all but off-limits. The public began seeing women reporting national news from crisis areas around the world, covering political conventions, speaking from the White House lawn, cohosting entire local news programs from behind anchor desks. Behind the scenes they became film editors, associate producers for hard news, full-fledged producers of documentaries. On the business side they moved into sales and program promotion and affiliate relations. Finally, toward the end of the 1970's, a few women managed to crack the hitherto impenetrable executive level of television.

In October 1978 Jane Cahill Pfeiffer was named chairman of NBC at a reported salary of more than $400,000 a year. Less than two years later, in a story that made front-page news, Mrs. Pfeiffer was forced to resign. In one sense her ouster was a clear sign of how far women had come in television. No account of her dismissal made anything of the fact that she was a woman. She had been hired with as much fanfare as any of the top men executives who had preceded her, and she had been fired just as suddenly and just as brutally. Television has always been a place where people are only as good as the latest Nielsen ratings.

These ratings are television's Bible. On the basis of approximately 1,200 American households, whose daily viewing habits are closely monitored by the A.C. Nielsen Company, the television tastes of the entire nation are determined. Each new season the executives in television-land await with fear and trembling Nielsen's verdict on their new programs. Since advertisers buy audiences rather than programs, a highly rated program with a large audience can charge its advertisers more than a program with lower ratings. If a network finishes a season with its programs averaging even one rating point over a rival network, this means an estimated profit of between $50,000,000 and $60,000,000. Television executives, therefore, are not in the business of rocking the boat when it comes to programming. They are in the business of giving viewers what the ratings say viewers want.

There is no reason to believe that the women of television will be any less in awe of ratings than men, not if they want to remain in this immensely profitable industry. If the ratings continue to reflect America's taste for sex and violence and mindless game shows, then that's what America will get — and women will be bringing it to them. Change, if and when it comes, must come from outside the industry rather than from within. By watching what it does today, the viewing public dictates what it will get tomorrow.

Men still run television, but women are there and they are making a difference, often in immeasurable ways. Moreover, in an industry that exerts such a powerful influence over the way people think and behave, it is these little differences that add up to a tremendous impact. When Fonzie of the situation comedy series "Happy Days" took out a library card on one segment of the show, librarians across the country reported a staggering 500 percent increase in library-card applications. So it is with women. When Mary Tyler Moore moved away from the traditional character of woman-as-housewife into the role of a financially independent working journalist, that made a difference. An articulate woman reporting the news from a crisis area in the Middle East can't help but change people's minds about what all women are capable of doing. And that makes a difference. When a woman produces a documentary or writes a screenplay, she brings her own feelings and sensitivities and attitudes as a woman to her work. And that makes a difference. It can make the character of a fictional woman real; it can make a woman's views have some influence.

Fifty years ago E.B. White assessed the coming of television. "A shining radiance in the sky"? he asked, or "an unbearable disturbance of the general peace"? Which will it be? The question is as valid today as it ever was then. Only one thing has changed. Now, if television ever brings us a more lasting radiance, it will be through the efforts of both men and women working together.

Renee Poussaint, anchorwoman for the evening news at WJLA-TV in Washington, D.C. *(Photo Courtesy WJLA-TV)*

CHAPTER 1

RENEE POUSSAINT

□ ANCHORWOMAN □

IN 1978 thirty-three-year-old Renee Poussaint was named coanchor of the six- and eleven-o'clock evening news for WJLA-TV, the ABC affiliate station in Washington, D.C. Shortly after assuming her new anchoring duties, the station's news director posed a somewhat startling question to her. "Renee," he asked, "are you a happy person?"

"What do you mean?"

"Well," he said, "I mean . . . ugh, are you an up, sort of bouncy person?"

"No," said Renee, rather amused, "actually I'm not. But you should have known that before you hired me. I'm *not* cute. I think I'm a likable person, a fairly mellowed-out person, but I'm not bouncy-bouncy."

Renee was right about herself. Cuteness is not her style. Very tall and slender, she is a strikingly attractive woman with an easy, direct manner that instantly conveys a high degree of intelligence and self-assurance. She has good reason for feeling self-assured. When she became the new anchor at WJLA, she came to the station with an impressive list of credentials. Before beginning her television career, she'd learned to speak fluent French, earned a master's degree in African Studies, taught college English, and had translated parts of the Bible into Swahili. In her five years in television, she'd gone from being a local news writer to a local news reporter to a CBS network correspondent.

Anchoring, however, is altogether different from reporting. Reporters are sent to various locations to cover the news as it breaks.

After writing their stories, they give what usually amounts to no more than fifteen-second stand-up reports in front of the camera. Anchors, on the other hand, host entire news programs from inside television studios. Their job is to announce the day's stories, introduce the various reporters, keep the news flowing smoothly, and sustain a level of interest that will hold viewers fascinated for an hour or more.

"When I first began anchoring," says Renee, "my coanchor, David Schoumacher, told me: 'You'll have to make a complete reversal from what you did as a correspondent. The things that are valued in a network reporter — aggressiveness, a hard-nosed attitude, objectivity, askings lots of questions — are anathema in an anchor. People want an anchor to be their friend — a stable, reassuring sort of person who doesn't make enemies.'"

These days WJLA's news director no longer worries about Renee. Half way through her first four-year contract as an anchor, she has become a familiar and respected television figure in Washington. Rarely do local news anchors have the kind of network background that she's had, and that is the reason she has never allowed herself to be cute or bouncy or bubbly in an effort to capture viewers' attentions. To Washington audiences, she is simply a very good journalist — articulate, direct, steady. Obviously at ease in front of a camera, she conveys her own natural warmth and charm without even trying.

No one who knows Renee is surprised by her success in television. On her mother's side, she is the third generation of very successful women. "My grandmother really broke molds," says Renee with pride. "She graduated from college with a degree in pharmacy and started her own drugstore in the little town of Humboldt, Tennessee. She did that at a time when few women, especially black women from small southern towns, ever went to college and ran their own businesses." Renee's mother, Bobbie Mae Vance, left Tennessee as a young woman and moved to New York City. There she met and married Renee's father, one of eight children of a New York City printer. When Renee was born in 1944, her mother was a social worker with the city's welfare department. Since then she has become the city's Assistant Commissioner of Human Resources.

As a little girl, Renee wanted to become a great dancer. Every Saturday morning her mother escorted her to ballet classes. "Afterward, my treat was to go to the drugstore down the street for breakfast. So not only did I get to take dance classes, but I got to eat out in a restaurant." She kept dancing for years, switching from ballet to modern dance and, finally, to African and Haitian dance. As a teenager, she spent three months dancing professionally with a Haitian dance troupe that performed in and about the city's parks, museums, and libraries. "That cured me," says Renee, laughing. "I saw then that I didn't really want to be a dancer."

What she did want to be she didn't know. She was a good student, however. After moving from Manhattan to St. Albans in the borough of Queens when she was twelve, she continued getting top grades in the city's public schools. She began thinking about college. "I knew I wasn't interested in a standard four-year education. I wanted something that would expose me to the outside world. So I applied to Howard University, Antioch, Sarah Lawrence, and Bennington." Sarah Lawrence, a small women's college in nearby Bronxville, New York, was where she ended up. "Of course," she explains, "I couldn't afford Sarah Lawrence. But at that time the college was running out of black students. So they offered me such a good scholarship that it ended up being the cheapest place I could go."

Same as B.W.

From the day she entered Renee knew that she wanted to take advantage of Sarah Lawrence's program that allowed qualified students to spend their junior year studying abroad. To do that, she settled on a major in Comparative Literature, taking lots of French courses and concentrating on both French and American literature. "I liked Sarah Lawrence," she says somewhat hesitantly. "Academically, it was very good and really stimulated my intellectual curiosity. But I'm not sure I would have lasted if I hadn't known I was going to take my junior year in Paris."

Part of the problem was that she was one of only two black women in a class full of very wealthy whites. "Two of us per class," she says sardonically. She smiles. "We were looked upon as sort of exotic folk, I guess. The other black woman in my class came from a family that had money, which made her more similar to everyone else. Since I came from a middle to lower-middle class background, it was harder for me. But after the first six months, I didn't feel too uncomfortable."

Renee was at college during the peak of the 1960's civil rights movement. "I was as involved in the movement as I could be and still remain in the North," she explains. Most vacations she worked for C.O.R.E., the Congress of Racial Equality. One summer she chopped cotton in the Deep South and lived with a black sharecropping family. After taking her junior year in Paris where she studied at the Sorbonne, she returned to spend her senior year on an internship with the legal defense fund of the N.A.A.C.P. Renee explains her passionate involvement in black causes very simply. "I don't think it was possible to be young and black at that stage and not be involved."

Following graduation, she went to French-speaking west Africa. Almost always speaking French, she traveled around Senegal, Mali, Guinea, and the Ivory Coast. She loved being in Africa and would have liked to have stayed beyond the summer, but that was out of the question. Months earlier she had decided that the best way of channeling her political activism and of helping disadvantaged Americans was to become a lawyer. One of the finest, most competitive graduate schools of law in the country, the Yale Law School, had accepted her as a first-year student. She had to go home.

Renee finished one year at Yale. "I realized I really didn't want to be a lawyer all that badly. Being a Leo," she laughs, "I decided it just wasn't worth it to stick around to graduate." She had a compelling reason for wanting to move on. In her senior year at Sarah Lawrence she had fallen in love with a young lawyer, Henry Richardson, who had been working for the U.S. government while she'd been at Yale. Knowing of her disaffection with law school, he had written urging her to join him in Africa. As an added bit of persuasion, he said that he'd met several men in the British civil service who had told him that if she came they would give her a job.

He was wrong. When Renee arrived in east Africa she couldn't find work. In Africa at that time it was not the custom for black women to work. The only women who worked there were white Europeans. Since Henry was very light-skinned, people had mistakenly thought that he was either Arab or Asian. Thus, when they'd assured him that his American fiancée would have no problem finding work, they assumed Renee would be white. "And then," she says, "I showed up—very black and wearing my hair in an Afro. Suddenly, there were no jobs."

At last, after three months of persistence, she found work selling advertising time for an African radio station. It was a boring job, not at all what she'd expected to be doing in Africa, but at least it kept her busy and helped pay the bills. It was during this time, while traveling in Kenya, that she first began to realize the awesome power of television. What were black Kenyans watching on their television sets? Imported sitcoms (situation comedies), reruns of "I Love Lucy" and "The Cisco Kid"! She was horrified. "'This is so wrong,' I thought, 'so totally inappropriate. There's no reason in the world why African kids should have to grow up with that.'"

Yet, at this point, it never occurred to her to think about television in terms of her own life. That would come later. Meanwhile she returned to America the following year. She found a job immediately with an organization in New York that ran a foreign exchange program, placing Americans in businesses abroad and foreigners in American companies. She stayed for a year. "It was good work, challenging and fun. It took me six months to get on top of the job and another six months to be innovative about what I was doing. Then I was ready to move on."

She couldn't forget Africa. Hungry to know as much as she could about it, she moved to Los Angeles to pursue a master's degree in African Studies at the University of California. She remained there for the next three years. In addition to completing her master's degree, she ran an African film festival at the university, edited an African art magazine, and wrote freelance art criticism. Also, she translated a book on African archaeology from French into English, which "I'll *never* do again," she adds. "That was one of the most excruciating tasks I've ever undertaken. It took me two years, working part time, because it was so technical that there were a lot of words even native French people don't know."

By now Henry Richardson had come back from Africa and was teaching law at the University of Indiana. Still very much in love with him, Renee applied to the university as a candidate for a doctoral degree in Comparative Literature. This time she wanted to explore African and black American literature. When word came that she'd been accepted into the doctoral program, she left Los Angeles and resettled in Bloomington, Indiana. There she divided her time between working on her Ph.D. and helping teach two classes of undergraduate English.

What should have been a fully satisfying academic life turned out to be quite the opposite. Taken separately, the two sides of her life, teaching and studying, made a lot of sense. But together, they made her feel conflicted. As a student, she was delving deeper and deeper into literature, becoming increasingly involved in such advanced, esoteric pursuits as translating parts of the Bible into the Swahili language. As a teacher, she wanted to communicate her love of literature to her students. But she soon realized that some of them could barely read.

"I began feeling that my own studies were separating me from my students, making me less and less capable of communicating with them. The ones who were functionally illiterate were mostly black students, and I cared about reaching them. It hurt me deeply that they couldn't appreciate black authors, the Langston Hughes, the Richard Wrights, and the Ralph Ellisons of the world."

She was particularly upset when she talked to these students about their reading problems. Why read? they asked. From watching a lot of television, they felt they were getting all the information they'd ever need.

Again, as she'd done earlier in Kenya, Renee began pondering the implications of television. "I still didn't know what I wanted to be, but I did know that my best talents were in communicating. Until then it had been in written communication — writing papers and articles and editing a magazine. But one of the things that had struck me in my black studies was the oral tradition. Black people have an oral tradition rather than a written one. I decided I had to broaden my skills as a communicator beyond the written medium. I decided to learn something about television because it was affecting so many young black minds."

In typical fashion once Renee had made the decision she didn't waste time. Sitting down one day, she compiled a list of fifty cities and large towns where she felt she could bear to live. Then, she wrote letters to all the television stations in those places. Here I am, she said in essence, a woman with lots of education, a few skills in some areas, and absolutely no experience in broadcasting. But, she added, that's why she was writing. She wanted to learn.

She got only three replies. One was from the general manager of WBBM-TV, the CBS-owned and operated station in Chicago. "I was told later that he had gotten orders from on high to begin hiring women in positions above clerical. So I guess he saw that I was literate and thought he might as well give me a try."

After driving to Chicago and meeting the general manager, she was sent on a tour of the station. She spent time in the news department, learned something about programming, and talked to people in the sales division. At day's end, she was taken back to the general manager's office.

"All right, dear, now that you've seen our various departments, what job are you interested in?" he asked.

"Yours," said Renee, not missing a beat.

The man looked stunned. Then he grinned. "I admire your guts," he said.

But before WBBM would hire her, she had to learn something about broadcasting. "Television stations are not training places," says Renee. "People don't have time. And they can get very impatient if you don't know what you're doing." Because Renee had gone on to say that she thought she'd like to be a news writer, WBBM agreed to be her sponsor if she could get accepted into the Michele Clark Program for Minority Journalists at Columbia University [now defunct].

Renee spent three months during the summer of 1973 back in New York attending Columbia. "If I hadn't taken that crash course, I couldn't have just walked into WBBM as a news writer. I would have started as a copy desk person. Also, having come from an academic background, I was used to writing tomes, taking all the time I wanted, and footnoting everything to death. Learning to write for television news was a whole reversal of my training."

When the summer was over, Renee went back to Chicago and started work. Like all television news writers, her primary responsibility was to write voice-over copy for the anchors to read and news stories that weren't being covered by reporters. At first she felt virtually useless. She'd learned a lot at Columbia, including the language of television, such as what words like 'key' and 'super' meant. But no training course could have prepared her for the pressure of being in a place where producers were constantly running up, handing her a stack of wire copy, and saying, "Okay Renee, read this. Then write me a story that takes no more than forty-five seconds." And there she'd be, knowing that she'd have to do what he said in fifteen minutes, because after that there would be another story waiting.

"You can't imagine the kind of stress you feel at first," says Renee. "There were no other black writers at the station, so that was an added reason I felt pressure to do well. The only thing you can do is just go through that initial period and painstakingly learn some of the tricks, how to read fast and get the main points, how to write in a conversational tone rather than an academic one. It took me four or five months before I became a decent news writer."

Renee became a reporter totally by accident. One day, nine months after she'd begun writing the news, she happened to be in the news room when a call came in reporting a fire in a nearby suburb. Since all the station's reporters were already out on stories, the assignment desk editor quickly pointed at her. All he needed, he said, was a warm body to go out with a camera crew and call the story back in to the station. But when Renee and the crew arrived, they discovered that they had a bigger story on their hands than just a fire. There had been a mass murder. A teenage boy had killed his mother, father, and sister and set the family house ablaze.

Renee raced to the crew's radio and told the station what had happened. "You're going to do a live stand-up on the six-o'clock news this evening," the producer told her.

"You're kidding!" she said. It was half an hour before air time and she was dressed in a scruffy pair of old jeans.

The producer wasn't kidding. He knew a page-one story when he heard it. The station had a live hook-up to the scene. With her there, WBBM would have a chance of scooping all the other stations.

"I was really scared," says Renee. "And I was terrible, just awful! I fumbled around, forgetting practically everything but my own name." That night she went home and tried to forget about it.

Bad news awaited her the next morning. The producer told her that when there was any follow-up to be done on a story, it was the station's policy to keep using the same reporter who'd broken the story in the first place. Reluctantly, Renee agreed to do her best. With every story, she got a little better. Still, she couldn't wait for it all to be over so that she could get back to writing.

"How would you like to try reporting permanently?" the producer asked her one day.

Renee was skeptical. "I don't think I'd be any good at it," she replied. "I'm not the kind of person who can run up to a grieving mother whose son has just been crushed by a truck and ask her how she's feeling."

"Oh, don't worry," said the producer reassuringly. "You won't have to do that."

But he was wrong. She did have to do stories like that. Like all local news reporters, she had to do any story the assignment editor gave her. Having never been trained as a reporter, she learned on the job and credits her camera crews for helping her the most. "Women reporters have to prove that they're not silly little girls or prima donnas. Otherwise, the crews can be quite cruel. But we got along fine. I took the position from the beginning that they knew more than I. They also knew that I wouldn't ask them to go into dangerous situations where I wouldn't go myself."

Stories involving physical danger were not the stories she dreaded most. One particularly difficult assignment was when she was sent to do a story on the recent resurgence of the Ku Klux Klan in Illinois. There she was, a black woman, interviewing individual Klan members and attending public rallies of a group famous for its violent hatred of blacks and its overriding belief in white supremacy. Even the Ku Klux Klan wanted her off that story. They promised the station that they would be allowed into one of their secret meetings if the station would send a white, male, Protestant reporter to cover it. They complied.

Another time Renee was sent to cover a union meeting of the Chicago Firefighters Association. The only topic on the agenda was how to keep women and blacks out of the union. All night Renee stood in the huge hall surrounded by four hundred firemen and her white, male film crew listening to insults to both women and blacks. Finally, it was over. Emotionally drained, she headed for the exit, trying to keep calm and poker-faced until she could get off by herself and scream. Suddenly, one of the firemen rushed up to her. "Renee," he said, having seen her on television, "we don't want you to leave thinking we're racists and sexists. But, well, it's just that the broads and the niggers are taking over the world!"

"As a black woman, I'm insulted that he could have said such a thing to me," says Renee. "But as a reporter, I almost felt flattered. He saw me as a professional and thought he could level with me."

No matter how she feels personally, she would never turn down any assignment. "Women reporters have been fighting for a long time to prove they're just as capable emotionally of covering any story as men. It's harder if you're a black or a woman because you're going to be exposed to more antagonism and hostility toward you. Professionally, you're supposed to be a neuter, always maintaining an impartial, unemotional attitude. Personally, that's impossible. But you can't afford to restrict yourself only to stories in which you feel no emotional involvement or you'd be restricting yourself too much. So, what do you do in a situation that's personally offensive? Well, I go home and pound pillows or something. Then I go out again and face it the next day."

Like most good journalists, Renee feels strongly about journalistic objectivity. "When I feel I've written a story where my own emotions might show, I always get two or three people who have nothing to do with the story to read my script. If they say my opinions or feelings are coming through, I'll rewrite. It's not my job to editorialize."

After only a few months of reporting, Renee was thoroughly happy in her new job. When WBBM gave her the additional work of hosting a weekly half-hour public affairs program aired at the noon hour, she was doubly pleased. This gave her a chance to delve even more deeply into the concerns and problems of the Chicago community.

In 1975, a year after she'd begun reporting for WBBM, CBS offered her a job as a network correspondent working out of New York City. It was the highest compliment she could have been paid, the dream of nearly all local news reporters. Renee's answer was no. The network was astounded and, as she later learned, not very happy with her.

"I felt I wasn't ready to be a network reporter, that I hadn't chased enough fire engines or paid enough dues. I didn't have any particular desire to go to the network, but I felt that if I did go I didn't want to be like some kid out there fumbling my way around."

She had an additional reason for turning down the network job. In Chicago she'd been making $34,000 a year. CBS wanted her to move to New York, which she felt would be more expensive, with a salary that would have cut her income from six to eight thousand dollars. "Their position," she says, "was that you should be so honored to work for CBS network news that money shouldn't be a factor." She wasn't buying it.

A year later CBS was back with another proposal. This time they wanted her to work as a correspondent in the Chicago bureau. Moreover, they said, they'd pay her considerably more than they'd offered before. Renee was delighted. The Chicago bureau was vastly different from New York's. The New York bureau had such a big staff of network reporters that many of them weren't given much chance to report and even less chance to get their stories on the air. Chicago had only six reporters responsible for covering the news in thirteen states. There were always more stories to do than people to do them. "Besides," adds Renee, "I knew the CBS Chicago bureau chief, Jack Smith, and I had enormous respect for him. I felt I could learn from him. As it's turned out, he's the best news man I've ever worked for in my entire life."

Frantic, exciting, exhausting—these are the adjectives Renee uses to describe life as a network correspondent. "You travel constantly," she says. "You get a call at 3:00 A.M. saying you're booked on a 6:30 A.M. flight to Detroit. They tell you to call them when you get there for the assignment. So, you keep a suitcase always packed and ready to grab because when you leave you never know how long you'll be staying or where you'll be going. You do a story in Detroit, then call the bureau chief who tells you to go on to Akron, Ohio, where there's a gunman holding some hostages. So you go to Akron, do the hostage story for three days, then you're told to go on to Cleveland. Literally, out of a month, you can be on the road for twenty-eight days."

Technical problems are always a headache for network correspondents and crews. Deadlines add to the stress. Occasionally the biggest story of the day will break five minutes before the national evening news begins in New York. Out in the field, the crew and correspondent know they can't make a mistake. They have one chance, and one chance only, to get their report on the air.

Renee feels that in certain respects it's more satisfying to be a local news reporter than a network correspondent. A local reporter has a chance to get involved in stories, seeing them through from beginning to end, learning something along the way. "As a network reporter," she says, "you're sort of a hired gun, here today and gone tomorrow, with no time for human involvement. It's bum-dee-bum-dee-bum-dee-bum," she adds, snapping her fingers rapidly. "You get very good at what's known in the business as quick-and-dirty stuff."

After Renee had been with CBS in Chicago for nearly a year, she made an important personal decision. She decided to marry Henry Richardson, her on-again-off-again fiancé ever since her senior year at Sarah Lawrence. By now Henry had stopped teaching law at the University of Indiana and had become the International Legal Affairs Policy Adviser for the National Security Council in Washington. Renee requested a transfer to CBS's Washington bureau.

The Washington bureau is huge. That was one of her problems. In Chicago she'd constantly been given assignments, maintaining an average of three stories per week that were actually aired on the national news. In Washington she and almost all the other reporters were on air much less than that. Moreover, the stories in Washington didn't interest her very much. "I was used to a more action-oriented, people-oriented kind of reporting. Washington is a one-industry town, government. Most of the reporting involves standing around talking to men in three-piece suits about the government."

Frustrated and restless after three months, she told the Washington bureau chief that she wanted to resign. Word of her unhappiness was passed along to the president of CBS News. He, in turn, told her that he understood her frustration and agreed there were too many reporters and not enough air time. But give it another six months, he pleaded. If things didn't work out by that time, he'd release her from her contract. Realizing that CBS had every right to hold her to her contract, Renee felt immensely grateful for his understanding. She agreed to stay for six more months.

Things did not change. They couldn't. The Washington bureau's problems were inherent to a news-gathering organization in the nation's capital. Within broadcasting circles, however, people had heard of Renee's unhappiness. The management of WJLA-TV, the ABC affiliate, asked her to join them as coanchor with David Schoumacher.

To WJLA, Renee seemed a perfect choice. First, she was black, and that was politic in the Washington market with its large black population. Second, she was a woman, a good balance for a male coanchor. Most important, she was an experienced television journalist with an impressive network background. WJLA recognized that they had something of a problem in David Schoumacher. He was too good, too well known. Because of his many years in network journalism, he'd had a tendency to completely dominate his less-experienced former coanchors. To prevent this from happening again, both he and the station had wanted to find an anchor with a journalistic background as strong as his.

As an anchor, Renee's life has changed dramatically. Nowadays

Renee with Ed Asner, her cohost for a WJLA news special called 'What
Does Your Mom Do?' aired on June 10, 1980. *(Photo Courtesy WJLA-TV)*

she doesn't get to the station until midafternoon. After checking the
day's stories and the news that's coming in over the wire services, she
then appears on screen at half-hour intervals to announce headlines
that will be reported upon in further detail on the six-o'clock news.
By five pressure builds in the news room. She and David
Schoumacher hurriedly begin writing or rewriting, doing most of the
top stories themselves. At six they are on. They read most of what
they say from a teleprompter, but also ad-lib when necessary to keep
the stories flowing smoothly. By seven the local news goes off. Renee
can leave the station, have dinner, do whatever she wants. But
shortly after ten she must come back to begin writing for the eleven-
o'clock news.

"When I first began anchoring, I loved having a predictable
schedule," she says. "For the first time since I'd been in the business,
I could plan my life somewhat. I actually could see my husband."

Basically, the anchor job involves reading the news, and that's all that some anchors do. That's not true of Renee and David. Not only do both of them insist upon doing much of their own writing, but both frequently revert back to being reporters, covering many of the major stories themselves. In addition, they often work on longer "soft news" stories that are presented on the news over a period of several consecutive days. "I find that if you function just as an anchor, the job can be deadly," says Renee. "To come in every day and sit down and read bores me to tears."

Strong news backgrounds are a must for anchors. She gives an example why: "Recently, I was on the air reading off the teleprompter and I came to a line that said the prime rate had dropped to 10 percent. I knew that wasn't true. A few days earlier the prime had been at 20 percent. It couldn't have dropped that sharply! Since I always check the news wire when I come to work, I knew that it had actually dropped to 19 percent. So I just inserted the correct figure. But that kind of thing happens all the time, and that's where news experience matters so much. You can't just be a performer or a news reader or you'll end up reading nonsense. News has to make sense."

The news director and executive producer make most of the important news decisions. They decide which stories should go on the air, which should be emphasized, and where they should be placed in the program. But often Renee and David have to make instant news decisions. If someone rushes up to them during the broadcast with a story that's just come in over the wire service, they can decide right then and there whether to broadcast it or not. If they can't make sense of the copy they've been handed, they won't use the story.

Few television figures are so constantly visible to the public as weekday news anchors. Twice each evening five days a week Renee enters the intimate setting of viewers' own homes to bring them the day's events. To thousands of people in Washington, people who have never actually met her, she has become almost like a close friend or member of the family. People care whether she's looking well or is wearing a becoming dress. They care enough to tell her.

"I envy men reporters because they don't have to worry about looking nice all the time. Women viewers can get very fixated on the accouterments. When I wore glasses, people called me up all the time to ask why I'd changed the frames. Or they'd phone when they didn't like the dress I was wearing. What I try to do now is dress with some distinction but as simply as possible. Also, I've started wearing contact lenses even though I prefer glasses. But I've realized that it's important to dress so that there will be as little distraction for the viewer as possible."

As a local celebrity, Renee is often asked to make public appearances. Neighborhood schools want her to be their graduation speaker; women's groups ask her to speak at luncheon meetings; civic organizations invite her to open day-care centers. Having always felt the importance of being involved in community affairs, Renee tries to accept as many invitations as she can. But with a working day that never ends until close to midnight, it can be exhausting to begin her day in the midmorning. "I've learned that I can have no more than two fourteen-hour days in a row," she says. "Otherwise, I get too tired and that shows on the air."

On balance, Renee finds it more satisfying to work as a local anchor than as a network correspondent. She loves the atmosphere at WJLA, the close communal feeling that exists there. Also, she prefers the greater involvement she now has with viewers and local community problems. She admits there are drawbacks, however. "One of the things you have to get used to when you go from network reporting to a local station is that you're not dealing with the same kind of resources. That's particularly true when you go to a local station like this one that's not owned and operated by a network. Out on assignments here, I had to get used to having only one camera and no producer. That was a big adjustment."

Still, the job of a local news anchor is one of the best jobs a television journalist can have. Renee is making a salary that is more than twice what she was paid as a network correspondent. And yet, much as she likes her job, it is difficult to imagine her remaining on any one professional plateau forever, particularly as she arrived at that plateau in her early thirties. So where does she go from here? What's the next step in television?

"Well, of course, that *is* the question," she says, laughing. "Theoretically, the only thing you can move to from local anchoring is network anchoring. But the odds against that are tremendous. There are so few places. And the odds are even greater if you're a black or a woman. Watch network news on the weekends. That's where you'll see all the blacks and the women."

"But each network has a weekday blonde," she adds. She ticks off the names of the three women who are seen most regularly during the week on network news: Lesley Stahl at CBS; Cassie Mackin at

Solid journalistic training is a must for any news anchor, says Renee. "You can't just be a performer or a news reader, or you'll end up reading nonsense. News has to make sense." *(Photo Courtesy WJLA-TV, Chicago)*

ABC; Judy Woodruff at NBC. It's no coincidence, she feels, that all three are beautiful blondes. "Men do the hiring. I don't know, maybe blondes are what they fantasize about."

Even if a miracle happens and she is asked to become the first black male or female anchor on network news, Renee is not sure that's where she ultimately wants to be. She thinks she'd really like to move behind the scenes, into a managerial position.

"Basically, on-air positions are powerless. Real power is in the hands of management, and in this business that is still very much a white, male world. I'm firmly convinced that the future for women and blacks in television should be behind the scenes, making the decisions about what gets on the air."

Renee Poussaint has gone a long way in television in a very short time, but her goal today is the same as when she was a fledgling news writer. As a communicator, she wants to have an impact on people, particularly on young black people. As a woman and as a black, she will never be content to be merely a token show piece.

Andy Austin, television artist for Chicago's WLS-TV, pictured outside of Cook County's criminal courthouse. *(Photo Courtesy WLS-TV, Chicago)*

CHAPTER 2

ANDY AUSTIN

☐ TELEVISION ARTIST ☐

"WHENEVER I SEE a crowd gathered on a street corner, I always stop. I have to find out what has happened. It's the same when I hear fire engine sirens. I'm the first one hanging halfway out the window."

Ann Collier Austin, known to everybody as Andy, shares the same impulse for being in the thick of things as most reporters and journalists. But Andy is only partially a journalist. Primarily she is an artist, as serious and dedicated to her craft as other artists who spend lifetimes in the solitude of an attic garret. When Andy works, however, there is never any solitude; nor are there windows through which her canvas is bathed in perfect north light; nor is there time to labor for days or months over a single piece of work. As the artist for the news division of WLS-TV, ABC's local station in Chicago, Andy's job is to capture the scenes and people of today's news, not yesterday's.

All of Chicago is her studio—its streets, its courtrooms, its hospitals, and funeral parlors. Lugging a huge black briefcase filled with sheets of paper, ballpoint pens, watercolors, and often her lunch, Andy goes wherever the station sends her. She draws fast—faster than most people write. She has to. If the most dramatic story of the day breaks in some courtroom in the early afternoon, an accurate re-creation of that event must be completely drawn and watercolored in time for the early evening local news.

As a television artist, Andy is following a long tradition in United States journalism. Sketches to illustrate news were used during the Civil War when hordes of artists invaded the battlefields on behalf of such publications as *Frank Leslie's Illustrated Newspaper* and *Harper's Weekly*. The development of the camera did nothing to end the practice. For one thing, there were places where the camera couldn't go then and still can't today. Most federal courts forbid them. Here, even a single camera with its clicking shutter and popping flashbulbs would be too disruptive. If television crews were permitted to bring their elaborate lighting and sound equipment inside, dignified trials could take on the quality of a carnival. The prohibition of cameras, however, isn't the only reason for using drawings. According to one veteran television reporter, "Drawings are frequently more effective than photographs. The artist can leave out irrelevant material — and the essence of journalism is elimination."

"When I was younger, the last thing I wanted to do was work for television," says Andy. "Artistically, the conditions are absolutely the worst — no light, no space, and always that pressure of a deadline. There have been times I've been so close to deadline that I've had to do my watercoloring while bumping down the streets of Chicago in the back seat of a crew car, dipping my brush in a used soda can filled with water held between my ankles. The car, with me and my half-dry sketch, would pull up at the station literally seconds before air time."

These days, all of Andy's doubts about television being the proper place for a serious artist have faded. "I'm totally hooked. I love my job! I've become so seduced by the news business that I know I'd never be happy working alone. Besides, I take what I do just as seriously as any artist off in some studio."

Being taken seriously is a refrain that comes up often in conversation with Andy. Perhaps that's because she fits so nicely into that old prejudice in which women, and especially very pretty women, aren't supposed to be taken seriously. Too, there is an appealingly vulnerable and sensitive quality about Andy that makes most people want to protect her. In this they are wrong. Behind the fragile appearance and rather tentative expression lies a woman of enormous inner strength, a woman who knows exactly who she is and what she wants.

It is a strength that has developed with the years. "When I was growing up, being taken seriously, particularly by oneself, was a difficult act of the imagination. For years I believed my ambitions were no more than schoolgirl fantasies."

Born in Boston in 1935, Andy was the oldest of three children. Even before she was old enough to go to school, she loved to draw. Her father, who strongly believed that the artistic life was the only one worth pursuing, was delighted. He applauded his tiny daughter's first doodlings of heart-shaped creatures with sticks for arms and legs who lived in families that did things together. Later, when Andy's artistic bent showed no sign of abating, he encouraged her to discipline herself by copying nativity paintings.

" 'Don't be a damn housewife!' my father was always telling me. '*Do* something. Be good at something.' When I was twelve, he took me to see a Hasty Pudding Show at Harvard College. There was a song in it with the line, 'I want to go places and do things.' For weeks Daddy and I kept singing that line around the house. I still love it—it's my credo."

Growing up, Andy never could quite fathom her family's financial circumstances. Because her father worked on a freelance basis, writing travel books one year, doing museum public relations the next, and not working at all sometimes, there were very good years for the family and very bad. There was a long period of time in Boston when the children had the best—servants, dancing classes, private schools. Then, when Andy was fourteen, the family went so deeply into debt that their car was impounded. After that, things seemed to get much better. At fifteen Andy was sent off to the Shipley School, a private girls' boarding school outside Philadelphia. By this time she had learned an important lesson. For her, the pursuit of money and financial security would always be an unworthy goal, unimportant and undependable. What really counted, the only thing that could carry a person through both good years and bad, was the development of one's own resources and talents.

But what were her talents? That was the problem. All through high school she wasn't sure she had any. Yes, she liked to draw, but her drawings were confined to the standard high school art courses and to doodling lots of faces of girls with perky, upturned noses in the margins of her notebooks. Besides, another girl at Shipley was generally conceded to be the school's artist while Andy's talents went unnoticed. "Actually," she says emphatically, "I don't have that much natural talent. Some people just draw automatically, which I don't pretend to do. For me, it's more a matter of training and motivation and caring—*really* caring."

Sometimes, caring too much can be counterproductive. When Andy graduated from Shipley and went on to Vassar College, she never took a single art course the entire four years she was there. "I was so afraid of its addictive effects, afraid it would take away from time I should be spending on other courses where I'd have a chance of discovering what I wanted to do with my life."

In this respect Andy differed from most college women of the 1950's. Few of them pondered how they would use their education. Making Dean's List and getting good grades were nice things to write home about, but real success lay in snaring a man. No honor that Vassar conferred upon a student could compare to a brand-new diamond engagement ring. But, insists Andy, "I really questioned getting married. I guess I saw it as something I'd probably do eventually because it was part of life. But I saw the dangers in it. And I always put my own life first."

In the middle of her junior year she suddenly decided she wanted to become a Latin American expert. "It was a dumb idea, typical of me then. I'd been in love with a guy at Princeton who was majoring in Latin American studies. After we'd already broken up, I decided to do the same thing as he. So I took all these Latin American courses, some of which were just me and the teacher. I wanted, possibly, to be an archaeologist. Except, of course, I never wanted to dig anything because I hate dirt and I'm afraid of snakes." Nevertheless, she did well enough at Vassar to be accepted for the fall after graduation into the Latin American Studies graduate program at the University of California in Berkeley.

That summer Andy went to Europe. It was her first trip abroad, a two-month interlude between college and graduate school. She traveled with friends from one country to the next. In Paris she sketched scenes of the city from the banks of the Seine. Never had she felt such an excitement and sense of freedom. It wasn't a question of not wanting to go home. She felt she couldn't, not yet, anyway. It was as if the whole continent of Europe was reaching into the very core of her being, tugging at artistic instincts that the more pragmatic side of her had long refused to acknowledge.

In the final weeks of summer, she frantically contacted consulates in several countries, asking each of them about educational programs for artists. She decided to live in Italy. After writing Berkeley to say she would not be entering graduate school, she cabled her parents that she planned to remain abroad.

"Come home immediately!" was all the return cable said. But it came back with such astonishing speed that Andy knew she had no other choice. Back in the United States, she spent six weeks pleading with her parents, trying to make them see how the summer had changed her. True, she couldn't guarantee that art classes abroad would ever lead to anything concrete, that she'd ever have the talent or even desire to be a professional artist. The point was, she argued, she needed more time in Europe before she could begin to know.

At last, relieved that she wouldn't merely be drifting around Europe, her parents agreed to let her return. But, they warned, all they could afford to send her would be one hundred dollars a month.

Cramming a few hours of Berlitz Italian lessons into her head, she was off to Italy that November. She went straight to Florence, the greatest center of Renaissance art in the world, a city that had nourished artists for centuries. Finding an inexpensive room in a small *pensioni*, she enrolled in art classes at the city's Academia di Belle Arti where the tuition was less than ten dollars a year.

Still, life was difficult at first. "I was struggling to live on less than five dollars a day and I didn't know anybody and couldn't speak the language." Shortly after arriving, she got very sick. Day after day she lay in bed with a high fever. Too weak to move, not knowing anyone from whom she could get the name of a doctor, she began thinking that if the worst happened, if she actually died, no one would even know about it.

Slowly recovering, she went back to art classes. By now she'd had to cut down expenses still further by moving into a shabby, fifty-cent-a-day room. Adding to her discouragement was the fact that she was getting absolutely no instruction in her art classes. "Occasionally, the teacher would come by, glance at my drawings, and say, *'Chè brava! Chè brava!'* But that's all. Not one iota of help did he ever give me."

Among the other students, however, was a handsome young Italian named Carmelo. Though unable to speak a word of English, he began spending more and more of his time with her. After several weeks, he admitted that he'd become hopelessly infatuated with the lovely young American who had seemed so alone and defenseless.

"We spent the rest of the year together," Andy says simply. "Without Carmelo, my life would have been impossible. There is no way to handle Florence without an escort and, besides, I learned everything from him. He taught me art history and he taught me how to draw and he taught me Italian."

She goes on. "We saved my money because his mother would send him sausages, stale grey bread, butter, spaghetti, and tomato sauce. We bought only olive oil and wine. By spring we had saved enough to travel. So the art lessons continued all over Italy. We never stopped drawing, always drawing from originals. That taught me more, I guess, than anything I've ever learned. We'd go to museums and draw original Michelangelos' and original Andrea del Sartos'. Or some days we'd pack some bread and cheese, catch a bus, and ride it to the end of the line. Then we'd get out, find a place we liked, and draw some more."

Both of them knew that this free-floating existence couldn't go on forever. He had plans for his life and so, by now, did she. She knew she wanted to make her living as an artist. Though it was sad saying goodby to Carmelo that June, she had already decided to apply to the art school at Boston's Museum of Fine Arts. This, she knew, was what she most needed now — good, traditional artistic training.

Based on a B+ mark on the art she submitted for her admission's portfolio, Andy easily won entrance into the museum's school. She took anatomy and life drawing courses, learned to grind pigment, and studied perspective. It was fun living again in Boston where she had so many friends. Shortly after she arrived, she was introduced to a tall, lanky second-year Harvard Law School student named John Austin.

From then on, she never saw any other man. It was as if she had met her perfect counterpart, a man so like her that it almost seemed eerie. Although John was training to be a lawyer, he was an accomplished musician and composer, a man who felt about music the way she felt about art. In June, 1959, she and John were married.

That fall Andy learned she was pregnant. John worked hard to finish his final year of law school; Andy never missed an art class the whole year. But in late May, at the exact moment that her classmates were taking the art history exam, she was in the hospital giving birth to a baby boy. Although thrilled by her son's arrival, she was disappointed by the 'Incomplete' on her final art school record.

The next three years saw enormous changes in the young Austins' lives. Following John's graduation from Harvard, they moved with their new baby to Washington, D.C., where John worked as an attorney in the U.S. Justice Department. A year later, he received orders to report for duty with the Army Reserve. Again they moved, this time to an army base at Fort Sill, Oklahoma. While there they both came to the conclusion that he couldn't go back to practicing law. He wasn't happy as a lawyer and probably never would be. Music, on the other hand, was everything to him. Finally, he and Andy made a big decision. When his army duty ended, they took their entire savings, $11,000, and went to Austria. There in Vienna he continued his music studies for a year.

During this three-year period, Andy did little but stay home caring for their small son. In Washington, she spent whatever spare time she had doing oil paintings, either portraits of friends or, while the baby napped, scenes from her bathroom window. At Fort Sill she had more time to spend on her painting because there were so few distractions. She even had a little art business. For five dollars a head, she painted portraits of some of the other wives and children who lived on the base. The year in Vienna, however, was a total waste artistically. Having hoped to go to art school while John pursued his music studies, she soon found that without speaking the language, she couldn't even manage to find her way around the city. Furthermore, over there babysitters didn't exist. So Andy stayed home. "I became the typical suburban housewife," she says with disgust. "I stopped painting completely."

When the year was over, John felt sure he was qualified to teach music. But where should they live? Having changed the direction of their lives so dramatically, it seemed wrong to retrace old steps taken in earlier years. Deciding that they wanted a place where neither of them had lived to begin their new life, they chose Chicago.

By now their savings were depleted. Moving into a cramped, walk-up apartment on Chicago's near north side, John wrote music, did some carpentry and window washing, and took care of three-year-old John Jr. Andy became the wage earner, working full time for a Chicago bookstore and, later, selling sportswear at a fashionable boutique. Financially, it was a rough year. And scary, because Andy knew she was pregnant again. One year after arriving in Chicago, however, John became the music teacher at the nearby private Latin School. That same month, September, 1964, Andy gave birth to their daughter, Sasha.

Again, she became housebound. Although able to afford a somewhat larger apartment, their budget was still too tight for more than an occasional babysitter. Still, John and Andy weren't complaining. If doing what they wanted to do meant doing without some of the luxuries enjoyed by their friends, then that's the way it would have to be.

But were they living the way they had intended? Certainly John was happy now that he was teaching and composing. But what about her? Although she adored her two children and felt strongly that they needed her presence during their early years, she felt increasingly frustrated at being so isolated from the world. Outside her window, out of view, American boys were fighting and dying in Vietnam; here at home thousands of people were becoming involved in the civil rights movement. Feeling that she was wasting away in unending domesticity, she remembered her father's warning: "Don't be a damn housewife! Do something!" And she felt guilty.

At about this time the House Un-American Activities Committee (HUAC) was holding hearings only a couple of blocks from her apartment. HUAC was a United States congressional committee that had been formed in the early 1950's at the instigation of Senator Joseph McCarthy. Its purpose was to investigate charges against individuals accused of being Communists and suspected of having plotted against the United States. Andy was appalled that this committee was still in existence. She felt it had already done enough harm, ruining the lives of a great many individuals who had been wrongly accused.

Driven by her own horror at the witch-hunting aspects of HUAC as well as by a still undefined journalistic sense, she began going to the hearings with her sketch pad and pencils. With no press credentials, it was difficult getting inside. Sometimes she'd get up before daybreak to be first in line for a spectator seat. Other days she'd join the line of protesters outdoors. One day a CBS cameraman who'd seen her waiting on the sidewalk in every kind of weather took pity on her. Motioning her to follow, he sneaked her through a back door and into the press section of the hearing room. Years later, long after she had been issued her own ABC press pass, she would always emphasize that it had been someone in the television industry who had rescued her on her first journalistic foray.

When the HUAC hearings ended, Andy continued drawing. Art had brought a new wholeness to her life, connecting her to the rapidly changing scenes and faces beyond her apartment. She drew old men sleeping in the reading room at the public library and other old men bending over chess boards on lazy afternoons in Lincoln Park. She sketched her own children glued to the TV screen and scenes of sunbathers lolling on the beach along Lake Michigan.

Suddenly, in August, 1968, Chicago erupted. Thousands of young people came to the city, hoping to make their passionate disapproval of America's involvement in the Vietnam war heard by the delegates who had gathered for the Democratic Convention. A horrified world watched as Chicago police clashed in bloody street fighting with these youthful demonstrators. Later, eight men were arrested, charged with having plotted and organized the disturbance. Finally, it was announced that Judge Julius Hoffman would preside over their trial in Chicago.

The Conspiracy 7 Trial, as it came to be known, was seen by many as a battle between old and new, the old autocratic world of Chicago's Mayor Richard Daley and the new order of young people pushing for change. Press people from all over the world flocked to the city to cover it. The night before the trial began, Andy was much too excited to sleep. Here it was — a million-in-one chance for her to sketch an event of real importance! Up before dawn, she was the second person in the long spectators' line the next morning. Finally she and about six other people were told to go inside. Clutching her sketch pad, she slid into one of the coveted spectator seats.

"You'll have to give me that sketch pad. No drawing allowed in here."

Andy looked up. Peering sternly down at her was a bailiff. "But I'm an artist!" she wailed. The bailiff wasn't moved. Stripping her of sketch pad and pencils, he casually walked away.

Desperate and miserable after that idle first day in court, Andy knew she must do something, somehow get herself into the press section where drawing was permissible. But how? Newspapers had already given this plum assignment to their best reporters. She had an idea. It was a rather crazy scheme, but she figured she couldn't lose anything by trying.

"I began bugging Judge Hoffman, phoning him, leaving my name with his clerk. Nothing happened. So I telegraphed him. I told him I was an artist who hadn't been able to work for years because of my kids. Well, it worked! Finally his clerk let me in."

Thereafter, each morning followed the same pattern. The men and women of the press, with their press badges, would file into their special reserved section in court. Andy, holding no professional credentials, would be ushered all by herself into the same section by one of the bailiffs. What went on in the emotion-packed courtroom was of equal fascination to her as what happened in the pressroom during courtroom breaks. Because cameras were not allowed in court, a vital aspect of the press coverage depended on artists' drawings. She studied these artists, noting how quickly and accurately they worked. Television artists always colored their drawings, most of them using chalk or felt-tipped markers while sitting in court. Almost all of them put the finishing touches on their drawings when they were in the pressroom.

One day while she was in the pressroom, Andy overheard Hugh Hill, a reporter for WLS-TV, the local ABC station, telling a colleague that the network's artist had just been pulled off the Chicago trial for an important hearing on the East Coast. Without an artist, he complained, ABC's coverage couldn't begin to compete with the other two networks. At that Andy went over and tapped him on the shoulder. "I'm an artist. I can do it," she said eagerly. Then she showed him the drawings that she'd already done of the trial.

ABC decided to try her. Starting salary, they said, would be fifty dollars a day, but if she was any good they'd give her a raise. Within a day, Andy was making seventy-five dollars. She discovered that drawing for television was "not much different from life drawing classes where you have thirty seconds to get a gesture." Using ballpoint pens to do her sketches, she carefully made notes to herself while in court about the color of clothes being worn by the principal figures each day. Later, after leaving the courtroom, she would watercolor her sketches according to these notes.

She never quite got over being terrified by her new job. Always there was the pressure of deadlines—constant, constant pressure. Also, she often felt bewildered, not knowing exactly how much detail to use for drawings that would eventually be transposed onto people's television screens.

"Back in 1969," she explains, "television had rarely made use of artists' drawings. There was a lot of confusion about the best way of displaying sketches. Even some antagonism about using them at all. Once, in those early weeks of the trial, I was in the studio when a

Always under the pressure of a deadline, Andy concentrates on her drawings while waiting in the lobby of Chicago's federal courthouse. *(Courtesy Leo Cummings, WLS-TV, Chicago)*

cameraman came in. He glanced at my drawings and said to the producer, 'You're not going to use that crap on TV, are you?'"

There were other blows. Probably the most visually dramatic moment of the entire trial was the day that Bobby Seale, one of the defendants, was ordered bound and gagged for his disruptive courtroom behavior. At that moment Andy was not there. She had left five minutes earlier and was on her way back to WLS with drawings depicting some of the milder scenes of the day. "Says a lot about my news sense in those days, doesn't it?" she moans. "You can imagine how I felt when I walked into the news room and was told what had happened!"

Luckily Jim Gibbons, one of WLS's top reporters, had remained in court witnessing the event. Over the phone, he gave Andy a minutely detailed account of what had occurred. From this telephone description, she produced a sketch that was flashed before an audience of millions watching ABC's national evening news. Later it was picked up by the Associated Press and run by *The New York Times* and *Newsweek*. Thus the episode became another of the many well-kept secrets of behind-the-scenes television. Although Andy insists that the sketch was "embarrassingly awful," few who saw it would have dreamed that the artist had not actually seen what she had drawn.

When the Conspiracy 7 Trial finally ended, ABC asked her to keep working for network news on a permanent basis. Andy turned them down. She was emotionally drained. The tension in the courtroom and the pressure of deadlines had been too much too soon. Now that she was being taken seriously and depended upon, she felt like backing down. Perhaps it was fear of failure. Or fear of success. She wasn't quite sure. What she did know was that she didn't want to keep on working for television.

Andy's resolve didn't last very long. One morning Peter Bordwell, the news assignment editor at WLS, phoned and asked her to do a job in Chicago. "He didn't know it then," says Andy, "but he soon learned that I'm someone who *can't* say no to an assignment."

More than ten years have passed since she went back to work. Primarily she works for WLS but sometimes does Chicago stories for the network. Every morning she eagerly awaits the phone call signaling an assignment. Working an average of four or five days a week, she is paid over one hundred dollars daily no matter what the job. Picked up for work by a WLS car and driver, she either goes to assignments alone or with a reporter. When her sketches are done, the driver delivers her back to the station where she consults with the news producer before doing her watercoloring. "In television," she explains, "you work for so many people—for yourself, above all, for the reporter, the tape crew, the editor, the writer, the producer." Clearly, she loves being part of a team.

Being a woman in her job has its advantages and disadvantages, says Andy. "I've never felt any discrimination within the television industry. Maybe that's because the two artists who work for the local NBC and CBS stations are also women who, like me, got their jobs during the Conspiracy 7 Trial. But I do feel that, outside of television, our profession is considered the lowest of the low, probably because we're both women *and* artists. When the three of us are together in court, people tend to patronize us. Lawyers and bailiffs are always

Andy frequently travels to and from assignments with the station's minicam crew. *(Photo Courtesy WLS-TV, Chicago)*

coming up and saying, 'Now let's see what you girls are drawing today.'"

"On the other hand," she admits without the slightest trace of coyness, "sometimes it's easier being a woman. I know I've gone places and gotten stories that a male reporter couldn't have gotten. I'll admit it — I'm not above using a few feminine wiles to persuade a judge or sheriff's deputy or policeman to let me go places that are ordinarily off limits."

Because she spends a great deal of time in criminal courtrooms, Andy has had some encounters with a few unsavory characters. Once a henchman of an organized crime figure approached her during a court break. "Do you have a husband?" he asked. Then in a menacing undertone, he added, "Do you *love* your husband?" Another time a gang leader strongly suggested that she stop drawing his wife, ". . . or else I'll break your leg."

Threats like these don't disturb her nearly as much as the pitiful scenes of human despair that make up the much larger part of her job. It was her assignment to capture the shattered expression on former Illinois Governor Otto Kerner's face the moment he heard the

Andy captures a single moment of courtroom drama in this drawing of a man who has been found guilty of murdering his wife, being sentenced by Judge Thomas Maloney. *(Drawing credit: Andy Austin)*

jury pronounce him guilty after his tax evasion and mail fraud trail. She has been assigned to go to the hospital beds of small children, victims of horrible crimes or accidents. More recently she covered the trial of John Gacy, accused of committing the biggest mass murder in history. There she had to draw twenty-one weeping mothers and friends identifying their dead son's pictures. "I find I imitate expressions," says Andy. "If someone's crying, I start to cry. That's why I don't like drawing crying people. Aside from the invasion of privacy, I get absolutely exhausted."

In 1976 John and Andy's personal life was shattered. Their son, John, a golden-haired teenager with a wonderfully promising life ahead, was killed in an automobile accident in which he had been a passenger. John and Andy had had him with them for almost sixteen years. For them and his sister, Sasha, it was a devastating loss.

Knowing that she had to try getting her mind off what had happened or risk going crazy, Andy accepted a television assignment the day after John's funeral. "That day I proved to myself that I really was an artist," she says. "I was in a complete daze, but I found that my hands and fingers were doing the right thing. Because of the

Andy's 1980 drawing of John Gacy *(right foreground)*, accused of committing one of the worst mass murders in history. *(Drawing credit: Andy Austin)*

years of training, I could still draw—about the only thing I could do."

Since their son's death, John and Andy have led lives remarkably free of equivocation. If anything, their commitment to each other, to their daughter, to their individual forms of artistic expression, and to their life together in Chicago have grown even stronger.

John is no longer an elementary and high school music teacher. Feeling that a college teaching position would give him more time to compose, he went back to school for three years to get his Ph.D. Already his music has been performed by a multitude of ensemble groups, as well as by the Chicago Symphony Orchestra.

In early 1980 Andy was sent out to sketch the arraignment of several members of the terrorist organization FALN, who were suspected of various bombings around the country. The scene was much as it had been at the Conspiracy 7 Trial: the defendants had to be carried into court; they shouted and tore up papers; there was kicking and fighting; and the audience erupted into a near riot. Andy was reminded of the old days at the Conspiracy 7 Trial when she'd been afraid of the radical defendants, the armed policemen, the near anarchy. But now, a veteran of so many different trials and difficult

In this drawing done at a trial for attempted murder, the intended victim *(left)* and his assailant *(right)* are pictured together in court. *(Drawing credit: Andy Austin)*

drawing situations and not-quite-missed deadlines, she didn't even feel rattled. In fact, she says, "I felt that being able to depict all this emotion and excitement in a drawing was a wonderful thing to do—the best possible way to spend my life."

Andy has only one worry: A number of states recently have begun allowing cameras into their courtrooms despite opposition from the American Bar Association and the continued resistance in Federal courts. "Cameras could become the norm," she says, "which means that I would be out of a job."

In such a talent-intensive industry as television, it hardly seems likely! Cecil Tuck, ex-news director at WLS, speaks for everyone who knows Andy: "In my twenty years of news, I've hardly seen anyone so universally liked and respected as Andy. She combines superb artistry with great professional dedication, respect for deadlines, and a thorough knowledge of how to adapt her work to the television medium. As a sketch artist, she's simply the best and the fastest I've ever seen."

Pamela Hill, Vice-president of ABC News and Executive Producer of the "ABC News Closeup" documentary series. *(Photo Courtesy ABC News)*

CHAPTER 3

PAMELA HILL

☐ EXECUTIVE PRODUCER AND VICE-PRESIDENT ☐

PAMELA HILL APPEARS rather fragile. She is a slender, small-boned woman with a halo of baby-fine ash blonde hair, a delicate creamy complexion, and enormous dark eyes. In her office where, likely as not, she can be found wearing an old shirt and a pair of faded blue jeans, she looks even more diminutive than she really is.

No doubt about it, Pam Hill's office is impressive. With windows on two walls, it is so large that even a massive desk, several side tables, four or five arm chairs, low, white coffee table, long couch, and bookshelves holding three television sets, rows of film reels and books don't make it look crowded. It is an office that befits the importance of its occupant. Pam Hill may look small and fragile, but she carries with her some very big titles. As well as being a vice-president of ABC News, she is the executive producer of the "ABC News Closeup" documentary series. Indeed, she is one of a handful of women in television who have made it to the top, who have succeeded in penetrating the powerful executive level of the industry.

Heading a staff of sixty, Pam oversees production of twelve hour-long "Closeup" documentaries each year. She is good at what she does. Her documentaries have won more prizes than she will count. Television critics consistently laud her work. *Newsweek* magazine went furthest of all. Praising her innovative and provocative techniques in the area of investigative television journalism, they labeled her the best documentarian in the business, the natural successor of the legendary Edward R. Murrow.

Naturally, Pam is pleased with her success. Moreover, having arrived at the top, she feels comfortable being there. "It's a great feeling to have that kind of independence, to know that there's something you do in the world that you get recognized for and paid well. I understand now why I always thought that men, as they got older, got better looking. The reason is that they were doing well. They had better jobs and were successful."

Her expression changes to wonder when she speaks about the outward symbols of her success, the rewards that come to top executives. "Riding around New York in a limo is a great high. It's not as big a deal as bringing a woman's values to the corporate world, but it's a rush, there's no doubt about it. Lately I've started traveling to Europe, looking at some of the documentary work being done there. It's quite a feeling to be over there as . . . " she lowers her voice and grins in self-mockery, " . . . as an *international business-woman.*"

Although she speaks about the glamorous symbols of her success almost as if she were taking part in a masquerade, when she speaks about why she has risen to where she is today, there is not a trace of wonder or surprise. Hard work is what did it. True, she admits, she had the ability; but she adds, "I've always had an incredible drive to achieve . . . and this crazy dedication to my work, always a willingness to work insane hours. I once went seven years without a vacation."

Pam's intense drive to be successful stems from a need she felt in earliest childhood. Born in Muncie, Indiana, in 1938 as Pamela Abel, she and her younger sister were the only two children of the town's Buick dealer and his wife.

"My mother was an immensely talented, sensitive, and intelligent woman. Like a lot of college-educated women of her generation, she was very frustrated by not working, frustrated to the point of always entering dress design contests and national writing contests, and winning them. But she put most of her energy and drive into my sister and me. She always, always brought us up with an intense sort of achievement orientation. We had to do everything the best, to the point that she was really driving us."

Mr. Abel also played a part in his daughters' development. An expansive, outgoing midwesterner of German origin, he was the first to cheer when the girls brought home a good report card or were elected to a class office. In his own way, which was much more easy-going than his wife's, he, too, was ambitious for his daughters. But, says Pam, "His ambitions for us came out of that real midwestern, Bible-belt, businessman's attitude of anything's-possible-in-this-country, while my mother's came from her own frustrations."

Mr. and Mrs. Abel had good reason to have big dreams for their daughters. Pam and her sister would have made any parents proud. They were pretty, bright, leaders in school, popular with everyone. For Pam life in Muncie, Indiana, was just fine. Everything came so easily and was such endless fun that she was horrified when her parents told her toward the end of her high school years that they hoped she'd go east to college. Pam balked. Her parents didn't let up. At last, thoroughly disgusted, she agreed to enter Bennington College in rural southern Vermont.

By now she had decided that one day she might like to be a painter. Bennington, a small women's college in the 1950's which has since gone co-ed, had a curriculum known for its excellence in the arts. Because the college had an unusually flexible and innovative study program in which students were expected to spend large chunks of time working or studying off campus, Bennington had earned a reputation for being decidedly avant-garde. That was all right with Pam. Since her parents were pushing her east, she felt she might as well go there. At least it was different. She left for college in the fall of 1956, totally unprepared for the shock she would undergo in the first few weeks she was there.

"I came to Bennington with this smarty-pants view of myself. I mean, I thought, having been a cheerleader and having worn the basketball captain's jacket and the football captain's jacket, what else *was* there to achieve in life? And I got there and realized that I'd never heard of James Joyce."

It was humiliating. Back in Muncie she'd been queen bee. Here at Bennington she was nothing. Why? Because she knew nothing, she decided. Nothing, at least, that really mattered. Nothing, certainly, that mattered to these bright, well-read, sophisticated eastern girls.

"I spent the next four years trying to play catch-up. I was forever spending my time in line for standing room at the opera. Any time anyone from the East mentioned the name of an opera or painting I didn't know about I'd write down the name and look it up later. Oh, I never admitted what I didn't know. Never! I'd hear a word used in conversation—*faux pas* was one—and there I'd be, standing around and wondering what in the world it meant. Later, in secret, I'd go and look it up."

Suddenly she was thirsty to know everything, to read all the books, see all the operas, and do it all at once. Now, too, she longed to travel. Every vacation became a good excuse for another trip. All over the United States and up into Canada she went. She spent her entire junior year at the University of Glasgow in Scotland where she explored the British Isles and Europe. "I was lucky," she says. "My parents always encouraged me to travel and to explore. My father took the view that if he could afford it, he'd pay for it."

Whether on campus or off, Pam credits Bennington for having made a lasting difference to her life. "It had an immense influence on me. It fueled all those drives for achievement that I'd had as a child." One of her teachers, a history professor, particularly stands out. "He really taught me not just to learn but to think—what independent judgment is all about. That's so important in terms of what I'm doing now. Having independent judgment and being able to reach independent conclusions are essential as a journalist." Feeling as strongly about Bennington as she does, it's little wonder that she was pleased when, in 1978, the college asked her to come back, this time to sit on its board of trustees.

When she graduated in 1960, no one would have thought Pam had the makings of a future college trustee. Having given up the idea of being a painter, she no longer knew what she wanted to do. Telling herself that she needed more time, she went off to Mexico with the intention of taking courses in Spanish and Mexican history. But the summer session at the Universidad Autonoma de Mexico was so cram-packed with other American students passing their time taking simple-minded courses that it wasn't a very stimulating place. Bored, Pam dropped out. She stayed on in Mexico for a full year, continuing to study on her own. "And," she adds, "I also did a lot of traveling and scuba diving."

While most people would hardly consider these pursuits a good formula for getting ahead in life, Pam sees her year in Mexico as just another part of her education. True, it was a privileged education. But when she compares it to the kind of single-minded, vocationally oriented education of so many of the people who are applying to her now for jobs in television, she is even more grateful for her own background. "I'm always very skeptical when I get resumes filled with television and communication courses," she says. "The best thing to do to prepare for a career as a broadcast journalist is to read a great deal and do a great deal."

When Pam left Mexico for New York City, she still wasn't sure what she wanted to do. For three months her parents continued to support her while she explored possibilities. "I had this blind idea that I wanted a *good* job and at that moment, 1961, a good job meant not being a secretary. Not that there's anything wrong with being a secretary, but I was afraid at that time that it wouldn't be an avenue up. That's not so true today."

Finally, a friend with close ties to Governor Nelson Rockefeller, then governor of New York State, suggested that she try for a job in the Governor's New York City office. With a letter of introduction, Pam applied and was hired. In the Governor's office were five other recent college graduates, all of whom were doing research on either domestic or foreign policy issues for Rockefeller's presidential campaign. Pam was assigned as a researcher on foreign affairs, working directly for Rockefeller's key foreign policy advisor, Henry A. Kissinger.

"I started as a newspaper clipper. Then I became a real researcher. Then, sometime during the four years I was there, those of us who worked on foreign issues acquired these lofty titles of Foreign Affairs Analysts, which we made up!" Pam quickly adds with a laugh.

Henry Kissinger, back then, was a celebrated Harvard professor who also served as a goverment adviser on disarmament and arms control. In addition, he was an important aide of Governor Rockefeller's, in and out of the New York office, drafting Rockefeller's foreign policy speeches and writing position papers for him. As one of Kissinger's researchers, it was Pam's job to research and write papers that he could use as background material. "Our papers were always circulated," explains Pam, "once he'd given his final approval."

Kissinger's approval, of course, was hard to come by. Nonetheless, Pam and the other young researchers viewed their boss as being something akin to a god. "We adored him, and we were terrified of him. He's had an enormous influence on me. He was so demanding.

He would never accept a paper until it was good enough. He just kept handing it back, making us do it over until it was right. We, on the other hand, couldn't believe how lucky we were to have such fantastic jobs. When we started, we'd just graduated from college. The year before, we'd been writing papers and paying for the privilege. Now, here we were, writing papers and getting *paid* for it."

In the same year that Pam began working in Governor Rockefeller's campaign office, she also was married. Her husband, David Hill, was a young advertising executive. Although the marriage ended in divorce a few years later, for a while Pam felt as though she were sitting on top of the world. She had a new husband, an exciting first job, and in 1962, a brand new baby son named Christopher. "In those days," she adds, "I was feeling quite grateful that my husband *allowed* me to work."

In 1965, Rockefeller's presidential campaign office was closed and Pam was out of a job. With her qualifications the logical next step might have been a similar job in either politics or government. But, says Pam, "I knew I didn't want that. It was considerably before the women's movement, and I didn't think there was much of a place for women in politics. Also, I didn't have a burning interest in politics. What I did have was a burning interest in the issues. I wanted to do something that combined my interest in the issues with my experience in politics."

One night, in the midst of pondering what kind of job that might be, she happened to be at home watching television. What she saw stunned her. It was a documentary, a documentary so powerful and provocative that she'd never seen anything quite like it. Presented by NBC, it was called "The Decision to Drop the Bomb." It was investigative journalism at its best, the story behind the story of America's decision to drop the atomic bomb on Japan in World War II. It had been made, she carefully noted, by a man named Fred Freed.

That very night, she decided that if she could make documentaries like this, then that was exactly what she wanted to do. She went to see Fred Freed. As luck would have it, he was just embarking on plans for a three-and-a-half hour documentary on U.S. foreign policy. Hearing about her job with Governor Rockefeller, he hired her as a researcher. "The transition I made into television was one of those perfect opportunities," says Pam. "My whole background was in foreign policy, so I just went from one research job to another."

In documentaries the job of researcher is an entry-level job. Working closely with Fred Freed, Pam learned as she went along. And what are the things a future documentarian must learn? "First," she says, "you have to learn to become a journalist or historian. Then, if you're good at it, you learn how to create film with dramatic pacing and structure." Clearly, Pam was good at it. From her start as a researcher, she soon became the director of research on a three-and-a-half hour documentary. In 1967, NBC promoted her again, this time to associate producer. Now she had more responsibility for all aspects of production, a hand in the research, writing, filming, and final editing.

Even as an associate producer Pam admits that it was often difficult being a woman in those early years of her television career. "There weren't that many women then, and those of us who were there weren't taken very seriously. You always felt that skepticism, particularly from executives. At that age, I didn't know much about the technical side of film-making, so I also felt skepticism from the cameramen and crews. It's interesting, though. Once I began to establish a reputation in this business for being good and for being professional, I never had any problems."

Rapidly she was establishing just such a reputation. For starters, she was smart. She also loved what she was doing. Finally, and perhaps most importantly, she had made a choice. She didn't want to be second best. She wanted to be a first-rate documentarian. To achieve this, she was willing to commit all of her energy and intelligence; to sacrifice all of her leisure time; to work brutal, back-breaking hours whenever it was necessary. In 1969 NBC promoted her again. She became the director of the network's hour-long series of documentaries, the 'NBC White Paper.'

For most documentaries there is no independent director. The core staff usually consists of a producer, an associate producer, and a production associate or researcher. These three people see the documentary through from its initial research to its final editing. The producer, with help from the associate producer, is responsible for both the writing and the directing. But in the case of particularly ambitious documentaries, such as the "NBC White Paper" and Pam's present series, the "ABC News Closeup," there can be as many as two additional staff members, a director and/or an investigative reporter.

After working half the night to meet the deadline for an upcoming documentary, Pam takes a coffee break in her office. *(Photo credit: Sarah Banker)*

Being director of the "NBC White Paper" was one of the high points of Pam's career in television. For one thing, it was an interesting period in American history, those final years of the 1960's. A new order of highly vocal and extremely passionate young people had emerged. All over the country they had taken to the streets, staging huge protest parades against America's involvement in Vietnam, crusading against industrial pollution, rallying on behalf of equal rights for black Americans — all of which, of course, couldn't have been better material for journalists and documentary film-makers.

"I did a lot of traveling then, going from one city to the next, doing one story on pollution, another on Vietnam, and so forth. It was immensely fun, sort of all play and no work for me, because I was doing a lot of the research and some of the writing, but I didn't have to do it myself." With typical modesty Pam omits mentioning that some very fine work came out of all the fun. One documentary she directed, 'Pollution is a Matter of Choice,' won two Emmys and a Dupont award.

Pam remained at NBC for eight years. For most of this time she was single, living alone with her young son, Chris, and struggling to juggle the demands of her work with the responsibilities of a single parent raising a child. Then she married again. Her new husband was Fred Freed, the man whose work had drawn her into television in the first place, a man she'd not only fallen in love with but who, more than any other individual, had helped her grow professionally. Her marriage to Fred, however, failed even faster than her first one had. It lasted less than a year.

Pam blames herself. "When I was younger, I never felt all that secure about myself. It was hard to figure out where I was as a businesswoman and whether I'd be a success or not while I was still trying to figure out where I was as a woman."

After her divorce Pam stayed on at NBC. Again she was promoted, this time to producer of "Comment," the network's weekly half-hour of ideas, opinion, and film featuring NBC correspondent Edwin Newman. Then, in 1973, ABC hired her away from NBC to be a full-fledged producer of hour-long "Closeup" documentaries. "And that," says Pam, "is what I really wanted to do all along — produce documentaries."

With her first assignment at ABC Pam began making a name for herself. She produced, directed, and cowrote a highly acclaimed documentary called 'Fire!.' The film, which included an unforgettable and controversial scene of a baby trapped inside a burning crib, was a horrifying exposé of why people lose their lives in fires. What viewers learned was that human beings have created for themselves a dangerously flammable, highly combustible world, a world in which the clothes they wear, the houses they live in, and the airplane seats they travel in, are a real threat to their lives. The documentary's message was tough. It blamed private industry for foisting so much hazardous material on an unsuspecting public. And it blamed the federal government for not protecting American lives by imposing stiffer standards and legislation against the production of this material.

'Fire!' attracted the third largest audience in the history of ABC's hard news documentaries. It also won two Emmys for best documentary and best direction, as well as the Peabody, Dupont, and National Press Club awards. Even more important, it resulted in some much-needed reforms in the production of commonly used material.

Pam's next assignment, a documentary on health care for the disadvantaged called 'A Case of Neglect,' proved that her first success hadn't been a fluke. She did it again, with *The New York Times* saying, "Miss Hill offered a powerful jolting of public conscience in bringing the causes and possible solutions up to date." As a documentarian, it was beginning to look as if she couldn't go wrong! In 1975 she produced, directed, and cowrote 'Food: The Crisis of Price,' which *The Christian Science Monitor* called a "shatteringly effective presentation of a complex subject."

It was an exciting and happy time for Pam, those years between 1973 and the end of 1978, both in her professional life and in her personal life. Professionally she was at the top of her form, doing what she'd always wanted to do and getting rave reviews for her work. Her private life, too, had brightened considerably. She had fallen in love again and, in 1973, had married Tom Wicker, a brilliant and charming North Carolinian who was a distinguished novelist, journalist, and columnist for *The New York Times*.

Pam took a chance on a third marriage because she realized that no matter how fulfilling her work was, it could never fulfill her totally. "I wanted to share my life in a way I hadn't before. I wanted friendships, dinner parties, a vacation now and then." She credits the success of this new marriage to the fact that she was older when she

Pam Hill and her husband, Tom Wicker, relaxing in the garden of their New York town house. *(Photo credit: Sarah Banker)*

married and felt more secure about herself professionally. In addition, she and Tom have much in common. They are both journalists, both committed to their work, both exceedingly successful. Says Pam, "The equalization of the relationship makes an enormous difference."

In 1977 Roone Arledge was named president of ABC News and Sports, becoming the presiding figure over all ABC's daily news programs, sports programs, and documentaries. As the former head of ABC Sports alone, he had earned huge profits for the network for such popular programming as "Wide World of Sports" and "Monday Night Football." ABC decided that if anyone could make its news division more closely competitive with that of the other two networks, he was their man. Six months after he assumed his position, the somewhat startling announcement was made that Roone Arledge had appointed thirty-nine-year-old Pamela Hill as the new executive producer of the "ABC News Closeup" documentary unit.

When he had first offered her the position, Pam had anguished over the decision. "I loved producing documentaries. I was happy doing it; I was good at it. I liked going on location and seeing an idea through from beginning to end. I wasn't at all sure I wanted to be an executive. But Roone came to ABC just as I was beginning to feel restless about the limitations of documentaries and thinking how *boring* they were. I had also begun to think more and more about what was possible, the kinds of things I'd like to do."

She knew she had no other choice. None of her restlessness would be cured by staying where she was. In order to effect change she had to have the power to make decisions and to carry them out. Happily she discovered that Roone Arledge had many of the same complaints about documentaries that she had. "Roone has immensely good instincts about production," she says. "His commitment to quality documentaries and ABC's commitment to him was one of those rare opportunities."

She and Roone Arledge began with certain premises about what kinds of change they wanted. They agreed on four major goals. The first was to restore the reputation that ABC had once had for good, solid, investigative journalism. Second, they both agreed that the format of documentaries, which hadn't changed in twenty years, had gotten monotonously stale. They wanted to try new approaches and formats. Third, says Pam, "I wanted to try using some outside producers. I didn't have the feeling that the networks had a corner on the market on good journalism." Finally, she adds, "I wanted more emphasis on all aspects of the craft of making documentaries. I'm from a generation of film buffs, so I wanted more emphasis on the writing and, especially, on the quality of film-making."

Even before becoming head of the "Closeup" unit, she had hatched an idea for a new kind of documentary reflecting these goals. Now, with Roone's approval, she went ahead with production, naming Helen Whitney, a talented producer she'd worked with in the past, to produce it under her supervision. Called "Youth Terror: The View From Behind the Gun," it offered an intimate and probing portrait of a teenage gang of hoodlums who roamed city streets preying on innocent victims.

Unlike the traditional format of documentaries, there was no well-known narrator commenting on the whys and wherefores of urban gang life and thus creating a comfortable distance between viewer and what was being viewed. Nor was there even much of a script. The camera did most of the work, leading the viewer into the midst of the gang, letting him listen to gang members talk about themselves, intimately involving each member of the television audience in the unrehearsed and horrifying bursts of violence that are a daily occurrence for urban gangs. When it was over, the viewer felt as though he himself had been the journalist, venturing alone into forbidden territory to uncover what it is like to survive on the streets on the other side of the law. As a piece of nonfiction, 'View From Behind the Gun' was as spellbinding and chilling as anything that could have been devised by even the best writer of fiction.

Under Pam's supervision this documentary was followed by others: 'Arson: Fire for Hire' was a hard-hitting investigation into America's fastest growing crime; 'Terror in The Promised Land' was a thorough probe into the complicated issues and goals involved in the actions of the Palestinian terrorists; 'The Politics of Torture' took viewers to the Philippines, Chile, and Iran to document the complexities of the Carter Administration's human rights policies.

In early January, 1979, a year after becoming executive producer, Pam was elevated to vice-president of ABC News. Though pleased with her prestigious new title, she makes it clear that in no way did it alter her primary responsibility. "The vice-president title doesn't make me a part of the working day-in and day-out of top management. The real daily management decisions about news are made by three men senior to me. My job is to push documentaries and to make the very best ones we possibly can. That's what the network expects from me."

Pam's working day has changed considerably from the time she produced her own documentaries. As executive producer, she is the one ultimately responsible for the success or failure of the twelve hour-long documentaries that are aired yearly under the "Closeup" name. Seldom does she go out on location any more. Now that she must supervise eight to ten different producing units all at once, there simply isn't time. She spends more time than ever in the editing room, consulting with each production team on the final cutting and re-arranging of their films. And she continues to travel a great deal, but here, too, there's a difference from the old days. Now, instead of traveling with a camera crew to far-off film locations, she's usually off to places like Los Angeles, Washington, or Europe. Her mission has changed. An important part of her present position is to keep tabs on outside documentary work that ABC might want to use. Also, she is constantly searching for talent, film-makers whom they might want to work with in the future.

She works closely with her staff of sixty, twenty-three of whom she hired in her first two years as executive producer. "I am so lucky. I came out of an operation at NBC which is quite bureaucratic and staid, where there just wasn't a premium on getting wonderful, bright talent. But here I have this *really* remarkable staff of gifted people on all levels from the producers right down to the re-searchers."

But can an hour-long documentary, in spite of the talent that goes into it, ever hope to get the same size audience as an hour's worth of entertainment? Pam responds somewhat equivocally. "Certainly. When they're done with flair, documentaries are capable of generat-ing significantly better ratings than they have in the past. We've proved that. On the other hand, we're very dependent on the time slots they give us. You can't put an hour-long documentary against one of the top-ten prime-time shows. An hour show on a serious subject can't compete against that no matter how good it is. Of course, if you wanted to program documentaries for high ratings, you could. But we're a news organization doing serious pieces here."

In the competitive business of television, where programs compete for ratings and people compete for jobs, the few who get to the top, like Pam, do not get there without some grumbling from those who don't. Though no one disputes Pam's place as a first-rate documentarian, it has been suggested that her spectacular success was due less to her own merit than to the important, well-connected men in her life who eased the way.

Surprisingly, this accusation doesn't seem to bother Pam much. "That's not totally untrue," she says, "I had a very important mentor in Fred Freed. He was an immensely talented man, *the* premier documentarian of the sixties. He taught me a great deal. I worked for him for many years and then I married him. My present husband, Tom, has had an enormous influence on me in terms of his good judgment. When I got this job of executive producer, there were lots of times when I was uncertain and felt a lot of pressure and sought his opinion."

She continues. "I find nothing so wrong with mentor relationships. I still have them all the time in this office with both men and women. But I don't think that either Fred or Tom—or any man— could have made the difference in my career in the final analysis because I've always had this crazy dedication and drive to succeed. Anyway, they didn't do it. I did it. The Emmys I won were won long after I'd broken with Fred."

Pam feels strongly that women who pursue professional success must be prepared to make some painful choices. "There's a lot of myth around about what's involved in being a successful woman. For instance, the myth of the superwoman. That's the belief that if you just organize it right you can have your husband happy and your children happy and you can have great dinner parties and also you can have tremendous career success. Well, I just don't believe that. No question about it, you pay a price for success."

She continues, relentlessly self-critical and touchingly honest in expressing how she feels her success has effected those closest to her. "I happened to have been divorced when my son was growing up. Until he was twelve, I raised him alone. And I was working hard, traveling a lot. So he was really alone with a babysitter a lot of the time. I wasn't there to give him the structure most children need. I would say, 'Do your homework,' and then I'd leave. But I wasn't there to see that he did it or to say when he couldn't do it, 'Gee, I love you and I know you can.' And he's felt that. He's felt cheated by not having me there all the time, showing him how much I loved him and giving him the attention he needed. And he's right to feel cheated. Because he was."

She goes on. "When I became executive producer, I told my husband, Tom, that I was going to take a year and a half and do everything I could to do the job well. For all practical purposes, I took a vacation from my family's lives. I worked most of the time— ninety hours a week. That was a big price. They weren't very happy about it."

Yet Pam knows herself much too well and is too honest to pretend that she's found any answers from the past on how to live in the future. "Oh sure," she says with a burst of laughter, "I'd like to see my family happy, and I'd like to be having those great dinner parties and have a wonderful job and be terrifically successful!" A moment later she is serious. "But I can't really set a model for anyone else. Right now I'm trying to arrange my life so that I'm not working those crazy hours. I'm trying to find a better balance between time with my family and time on the job. But I don't know that a woman as driven as I am can really ever find that balance. I'm afraid it's never going to be ideal."

One final question: What about taking a period of time, maybe even a couple of years, away from work?

Pam reacts instantly. "Oh, no," she says softly, clearly horrified. "I'd go crazy—absolutely crazy. I never could imagine not working now. I find it much too exciting. I guess that's because I've finally reached the point in my life where I really have a sense of what's possible."

CHAPTER 4

CARMEN CULVER

□ TELEVISION SCREENPLAY WRITER □

CARMEN CULVER SAT IN CLASS and held her breath. The screenplay writing course that she had enrolled in weeks earlier was nearly over. Until now she had spent most of the time listening to what the other students had written. Finally she had submitted something. It wasn't much, just the barest outline for a screenplay that she had been mulling over in her mind for some time. In it she had sketched the story of a young woman named Willa, a woman with a rather startling ambition. Willa wanted to become a cross-country truck driver.

The teacher finished reading her outline aloud to the class, then tossed it back on his desk. Nervously Carmen awaited the verdict. "Can any of you imagine wanting to go see a film with a plot like this?" the teacher asked.

Silence. No one said a word. Not one hand went up. Obviously neither the teacher nor any of the students felt that her story had even the slightest possibility.

Carmen doesn't have to reach very far back into her memory to describe that scene of rejection. It happened in 1975. At the time, she was an impoverished thirty-five-year-old former college English teacher and the brand new mother of twin girls. The fact that she was in a screenwriting course was something of a fluke. She had intended to sign up for a course in writing novels but had discovered that the novel course met at a time that didn't fit into her schedule. So she had settled for screenwriting, though in her wildest dreams she couldn't imagine herself ever becoming a screenwriter. Says she, "I always thought that screenwriting was something done by people wearing Gucci shoes."

Carmen Culver, busy and successful West Coast television screenwriter.

These days Carmen still doesn't own a pair of Gucci shoes even though she could easily afford a whole closet full. When her classmates rejected the story of Willa, she was determined to prove them wrong. She went on and developed the idea into a screenplay that eventually became a two-hour television feature film. Since then, her life has rivaled the best of Cinderella stories. From her home in Encino, California, she continues to turn out successful screenplays with remarkable regularity. She is paid well for her work—a good deal more than $100,000 for each screenplay she writes. In the 1979–1980 television season, four of her screenplays accounted for nine hours of prime-time television entertainment, something of a record for screenwriters and a feat that makes Carmen one of the hottest new television writers around.

"I'm afraid I'm what you must call a 'late-bloomer,'" she laughs, marveling at all that has happened to her in so short a time. "Secretly, I had always wanted to be a writer, but I never wrote anything after the age of eighteen. I guess I was afraid people would laugh at me. Writing seemed such an impractical thing to do."

Carmen is a life-long westerner. She was born in Stillwater, Oklahoma, on July 28, 1939, spent her earliest years moving from Oklahoma to Texas to New Mexico to Missouri and finally to southern California, where she has lived ever since. The reason that her parents, Marye and Orval McGurk, moved so frequently when she and her older sister, Carol, were little was that her father was a government control tower operator whose job took him from one remote government-owned airfield to the next. When Carmen was nine, the family settled down permanently in Ontario, California, where Mr. McGurk went into the real estate business.

Carmen's interests as a child were what one might expect of a future writer. First, she loved to read — vitally important for anyone who hopes to go on and write. And write she did. Even as a very little girl she scrawled out poetry, stories, and plays. Besides doing a lot of reading and writing, she was a good athlete, an excellent student, and a child whose favorite weekend treat was a ticket to the movies.

Not until she got to Chaffey High School in Ontario, however, did she discover how little she really knew. Suddenly, she wanted to explore a whole range of things that hadn't even occurred to her earlier. Her high school French teacher, Max Vaucher, further stimulated her curiosity. "I loved French; and he opened up the door to a body of literature and a whole way of life in which I knew that I wanted, somehow, to be involved."

Carmen feels, too, that the religious training she got in high school was important. "It wasn't rigorous training, but I did come to know the Bible a bit. I am not a religious person; but I am convinced that it is very important for a writer to be conversant with Christianity. Not because I feel it to be superior to other religions, but because it has informed the history of Western literature so markedly. I only wish I knew more of the other great religions of the world."

By the time Carmen graduated from high school, she had stopped writing. Still not sure what she wanted to do with her life, she knew only one thing: she loved learning, loved the world of abstract ideas and scholarship that existed in school. And so she remained in school. Throughout the 1960's she spent most of her time as a student at the University of California in Los Angeles. First, she got her B.A. with a major in English Literature and a minor in French. Next, she earned a master's degree in English Literature. Finally, in 1970, she was awarded a Ph.D. in Education.

"As I see it now, I kept going to school principally because I did it so well. As a B.A., I hadn't the faintest notion of what I wanted to do with my life — a fact that now seems incredible to me, but there it is. Worse yet, as a Ph.D., I wasn't very interested in what I had qualified myself to become."

She had become Professor McGurk, qualified for a teaching position at the most advanced and prestigious level. At U.C.L.A. and later at the University of Southern California, she taught both English composition and Education courses. That was the part she liked — the working with ideas and the rewards of being able to impart something to a student that opened new doors to understanding. Other aspects of life in academia she loathed. Outside of class she saw entirely too much pettiness, narrow-mindedness, and political jockeying for advancement among members of the university faculty. "And ultimately," she adds, "I felt I could make very little impact. I want our schools to be better, yes; but I couldn't see how I, personally, could contribute very much to that goal. There's a lot of conservatism there, and a lot of interference from government at all levels. I wasn't happy."

When Carmen was thirty-three, she married. Her husband, Calvin Culver, was a design engineer at a large, well-established company. Carmen kept working. By now she had temporarily stopped teaching to become an independent consultant to several large-scale experimental educational programs funded by the U.S. Office of Education. Two years later, however, she had to take a leave-of-absence from this work. She and Calvin had become the parents of not just one baby but two — twin girls they named Cordelia and Jordan.

Nothing could have prepared Carmen for the way she felt following the birth of her babies! It was the single most creative and joyous event she had ever experienced. Somehow she felt different than she had before — stronger, more sure of herself, less willing to compromise with any aspect of her life. Although she had always wanted to go back to work once the twins were a little older, she began to dread returning to the field of education. Wasn't it wrong, she asked herself, to keep on doing something she didn't even like? For the first time in seventeen years she found herself wondering about the possibility of trying to be a writer.

Carmen Culver

It was the worst possible time to be thinking of changing careers, especially changing to something as financially doubtful as writing. Since their marriage two years earlier, the Culvers had lost whatever savings they had in unwise stock market decisions. In addition, Calvin had recently left his secure job and taken the considerable risk of forming his own company. The twins had arrived at a time when Carmen and Calvin had never been poorer.

Yet Carmen was in no mood to play it safe. Once she had made up her mind that she wanted to write, nothing could deter her. "I made a decision. I decided to spend every bit of extra money that we had on hiring a housekeeper, even though it meant going without buying one new dress or pair of shoes for two years." With someone to help care for the twins, she enrolled in a screenwriting course. Screenwriting happened to be the only creative writing course she could find that didn't fall smack in the middle of the times she knew she would be nursing the twins.

Looking back, Carmen is not so sure that the course helped her much. "It introduced me to some of the technicalities of screenwriting. But it didn't provide an entree into the business; nor did it teach me to write. It's a cliché, but no one can teach you to write."

"The film schools are packed with students; and certainly some of them have gone on to be very successful in the business. But it is not clear that their success is related to their training. Also, with some of them, I've noted the rather disturbing tendency to borrow from old movies rather than writing from life. That's why I think that rather than taking a screenwriting course it might be more profitable to use the same amount of time and effort in learning as much as possible about the history of Western culture and, simply, about what makes people tick. Certainly I wouldn't let the inability to go to film school or to take a screenwriting course stop me if I really wanted to write. In screenwriting, the buyer is looking for a good screenplay. He does not stop to read the writer's resume first. Nor is he as concerned about correct form as most aspiring writers fear."

At about the same time that her course ended, Carmen heard of a screenwriting conference to be held by Sherwood Oaks, a respected Hollywood film school. As part of the conference, there was to be a screenwriting contest. Already, aspiring writers across the country had begun submitting their scripts.

Carmen desperately wanted to take part in the contest. But could she do it? Could she take her idea about the woman trucker, turn it into a screenplay, and submit it in time? It seemed very doubtful. The date that all manuscripts had to be submitted was less than three weeks away. Not only had she not yet written a word, but in spite of the screenwriting course, she had never laid eyes on a completed screenplay. She did not have the vaguest idea what one looked like. Finally, even if she worked all the time, she knew she couldn't just take a leave of absence from the twins. They were only a few months old and she was still nursing them.

"Go ahead! . . . Just do it! . . . Start writing!" Calvin kept telling her. And so she did.

Knowing there would be no privacy at home, she chose a bench in a nearby park for her "office." After borrowing some completed scripts from the Sherwood Oaks's library to give her some idea of the correct form of a screenplay, she began. Frantically, obsessively, she kept writing. Every three hours she raced home to nurse the twins. But when their feedings were over, she was back on her park bench, writing some more. Public parks, she discovered, are not the most ideal places for privacy. On one occasion a rather sinister man kept hovering around, terrifying her with his lewd suggestions. One morning, just as she was arriving for the day, a very large, ferocious dog bounded up to her car, trapping her inside for nearly an hour.

Carmen completed *Willa* in two-and-a-half weeks exactly — just in time to meet the deadline. It was an unusual screenplay, mostly because it portrayed the central figure, a woman, very differently from how most women had been portrayed in the past. Typical female figures were usually very feminine and rather passive people whose happiness depended on having some strong, intelligent, handsome man around. Willa was as strong-minded, independent, and adventurous as any man. Her happiness didn't hinge on any other person; it depended on fulfilling her own personal goals.

"I chose trucking as her goal because that is, perhaps, the staunchest male stronghold. The theme of the play was power and autonomy. Willa is faced with a society whose expectations of women make it very hard for her to attain her goal. And in the end, she doesn't entirely "win." She's become a truck driver, but she has to sacrifice a great deal for it — and she's not completely sure that the sacrifices were worth it."

Throughout the summer of 1975, Carmen waited for the finalists to be announced. While waiting, she heard some encouraging news. Although no one knew who would emerge the winner, some of the judges had read *Willa* and were enthusiastic. One of them was Tony Bill, the producer of *Taxi Driver*, starring Robert DeNiro. He told her that he felt her screenplay had excellent chances for commercial success.

Because of the building interest in *Willa*, Carmen began looking for an agent. Nearly all professional writers have agents, no matter what kind of writing they do. Agents have contacts in the publishing and film world that individual writers don't have. Agents circulate their writers' work, oversee sales, and try to get the most money for their writers that they can. Producers and publishers usually take notice when a manuscript comes in from an agent, knowing that probably it will be a thoroughly professional piece of work. When a manuscript comes in unsolicited, sent in by an unknown author and without an agent's name attached to it, it is regarded with a good deal of skepticism. Says Carmen, "You can't sell without an agent — and you can't get an agent unless you have sold. That's the rub."

Carmen had even more need for an agent than most fledgling writers. In the fall, she and Calvin were leaving for Italy, taking the babies with them. Even though they were still in terrible financial shape, they had decided to all go because Calvin's new business demanded that he be abroad for an extended period. Knowing that she would be out of the country for a few months, Carmen wanted to have someone representing her just in case something came up about *Willa*.

She telephoned a friend for advice, an established screenwriter whose agent was the well-known Norman Kurland. "Oh," said her friend, "Norman is much too busy to take on unproven writers like you. But I'll call him and tell him that you're a friend of mine and that you'll be phoning him. Then maybe he can give you the name of an agent who is just starting out, someone who is still looking for clients."

That was good enough for Carmen. She waited a few days before calling Norman Kurland. "*Whom* did you say you are?" his voice boomed back at her with obvious impatience. Her heart sank as she realized that her friend had forgotten all about his promise. Quickly she told Mr. Kurland a little about herself, told him, too, about *Willa*. At last, more to get her off the phone than anything else, he agreed to see her.

But he did not agree to read *Willa*, not even when he met with her. That would be asking too much, he said. When she mentioned her upcoming trip to Italy, however, his eyes lit up. He told her that he had been collecting a special kind of Italian dinner plates, a kind he'd only seen in Italy. If she could somehow manage to bring him back one, well, in that case, he thought he'd have to do her the return favor of reading her screenplay.

Finding Norman Kurland's dinner plates. That became Carmen's sole mission in Europe! She looked everywhere. She came down with a serious case of pneumonia, was ordered to bed for a few weeks, recovered, and kept looking. Finally, just before returning to America, the Culvers wandered into a tiny restaurant in northern Italy. There they were! Carmen offered to buy a few. The owner said they were not for sale. Carmen finished her meal, picked up one of the plates, quietly slid it under her coat, and walked out.

Back in Los Angeles she phoned Mr. Kurland and, breathlessly, announced her return. "*Who* is this?" he shouted, apparently not having the slightest recollection of having met her. With that, she exploded. Laughingly, she told him how she had risked life and limb and imprisonment in a foreign jail just for the sake of a plate!

By now, *Willa* had been named winner of the Sherwood Oaks's screenwriting contest. Not only that but while she'd been gone, Norman Kurland actually had read it and liked it. In fact, he had already sent it around to several important producers and had some exciting news for her. Aaron Spelling, the producer of the hit TV series "Charlie's Angels" had taken an option on it, hoping to make it into a television feature film.

An option on a screenplay is a far cry from actual production. All it means is that a producer likes it enough to put a certain amount of money into buying an option so that other producers can't make it first. But producers like lots of scripts; they produce only a fraction of those they option. A screenplay that is actually produced depends on far more than a producer's initial enthusiasm. It depends on getting a star, a director, and someone to distribute the film after it's been made.

Still, it was a very big step for Carmen. On the strength of *Willa* she was invited to bring in ideas for Aaron Spelling's new television series "Family."

Proposing ideas for possible television movies or segments of an ongoing, prime-time series is part of what all West Coast screenwrit-

ers do. In the language of show biz, this process is called "pitching."
The writer meets with story editors, producers, or film executives
and pitches, or presents, ideas for future productions. "I've never
gone to any of those meetings without bringing with me copious
notes representing a tremendous amount of research," says Carmen.
"For Hollywood, I guess I'm unusual in that respect. People always
seem so amazed by how seriously I take it all. But it's worked for me.
I've never gone in to pitch ideas without coming away with an
assignment."

For "Family" she brought with her ideas for six separate, hour-
long segments. All of them were turned down. Still, the story editors
were so impressed by her research and understanding of the series
that they assigned her to write a segment for "Family" using an idea
that they'd already had. For this she was paid $15,000.

More important, she was suddenly being treated by people in the
business as a serious screenwriter. Next she contracted to write a
segment for the now-defunct series "The Fitzpatricks." Shortly
after that, she was asked to rewrite a story that had been written by
Joan Tewkesbury.

"I got all those writing assignments for one reason," says Carmen. "A lot of different producers had read *Willa*. So actually *Willa*
was my calling card—nay, the *only* sample of my work at that time.
The moral is that if you want to be a screenwriter the first thing you
must do is sit down and write a screenplay. All else is emptiness and
folly. This sounds obvious, but I have talked to hundreds of aspiring
writers, most of whom seem stunned by the news. The hard fact is
that no one will listen to you when you say you can write. You must
show them that you can by handing them a finished work."

One day, well before anything she had written had been aired,
Norman Kurland casually mentioned that the producer, Phillip
Barry, might be calling her. Mr. Barry, he explained, had read *Willa*,
liked it, and was looking for a writer to adapt a best-selling book into
a television feature film starring Mary Tyler Moore. The book,
written by NBC News correspondent Betty Rollin, was called *First,
You Cry* and was a touching, personal account of the author's battle
with breast cancer.

Carmen was so excited that she couldn't think of anything else.
True, her agent had only said that Mr. Barry *might* call—not much to
base her hopes on. But on the offhand chance that he did call, she

wanted to be ready. First she read the book and loved it. Then, realizing that she'd never seen the legendary Mary Tyler Moore perform, she planted herself in front of the television set to watch several segments of "The Mary Tyler Moore Show." When the phone call finally came with Mr. Barry on the other end, Carmen had already written the screenplay *First, You Cry,* in her head.

Turning somebody else's book into a screenplay can be tricky. "The greatest difficulty in adapting a book," says Carmen, "is making what is interior in the book externalized and visible in action on the screen. For example, the feelings of the protagonist, which he may express in the book via an essay, so to speak, must be translated for the screen. So you may give him a friend to whom he expresses those feelings; or better, you figure out how someone who feels as he does would *behave*."

Phillip Barry liked her ideas for *First, You Cry* and hired her to begin a process that all relatively unknown screenwriters must go through. First, he hired her to do only a story line. Then, because he liked that, he agreed to pay her additional money to write a more

Carmen Culver (before cutting her hair) with Philip Barry, son of the playwright, and Producer of "First, You Cry"

detailed outline, which is called a "treatment." After approving her treatment, he paid her to write a first draft. Then, a second draft. And so on until the script had been completed, approved, revised, and was ready for production. An approved final script, however, is no guarantee that a television screenplay will be aired. Far from it. Only one out of ten paid-for scripts ever makes it onto the air waves.

While working on *First, You Cry*, Carmen met and talked with Mary Tyler Moore many times. She met Betty Rollin only once, and then very briefly. "I didn't want to get to know Betty because that would have confused me. I had to think of Mary Tyler Moore as the central character, not the real Betty Rollin."

First, You Cry was aired on CBS in 1978—three years after Carmen had begun working on it. It received a great deal of publicity, rave reviews, and, ultimately, a number of Emmys in several categories. By the time television viewers saw it, Carmen had gone on and completed several other screenplays. Indeed, she had become a very busy and thoroughly professional screenwriter.

Among these new credits was *When She Was Bad*, an original screenplay dealing with the serious problem of child abuse. David

Carmen Culver (right) with Mary Tyler Moore and George Schaffer, Director of "First, You Cry"

Ladd, one of the top executives in the film business, had wanted her to write the story for his wife, actress Cheryl Ladd. "I did a lot of research for this one; I spent a couple of months at a child-abuse center. The story dealt with the causes and effects of abuse upon the whole family. What I was up against was writing about a beautiful woman who was an abuser."

When She Was Bad, a title Carmen hates, was broadcast by ABC. Most of the reviews were favorable, although many television critics felt that Cheryl Ladd was not up to the role. "I thought Cheryl did a nice job and was criticized unfairly," adds Carmen.

Her next screenplay was an original nativity story, filmed in the Middle East in September, 1979, and aired three months later at Christmas. Called *Mary and Joseph: A Story of Faith*, it took the view of Mary and Joseph as young teenagers in what Carmen feels was an historically probable situation. Again, she did a great deal of research and felt pleased with her final script. She was horrified by the production. "I sat down and cried when I saw what they'd done. They had a huge budget—$6,000,000. But it was wasted."

Carmen's unhappiness with the production is an emotion shared by most screenwriters at one time or another. After a writer has been paid for a completed script, the producer has sole responsibility for what happens to it. Whether the writer has any further involvement during the production depends largely on the individual producer. Says Carmen, "Ideally, I would be on the set, to make changes if necessary, or to fight for the integrity of the story. This "fight" isn't always because the producer and director are evil or boorish. The fact is—as egoistic as it sounds—the writer is usually the only individual who really knows every part of the story being filmed."

Meanwhile Carmen was too busy writing to spend much time brooding over one poor production. Besides this, her film credits were piling up. Best of all, *Willa* had been produced and was aired during the 1979–1980 television season. For two years it had seemed that *Willa* would remain nothing more than a much-praised screenplay, a script filed away and gathering dust in Aaron Spelling's inner offices. Finally Mr. Spelling had sold his option on it to another producer, Michael Viner. Mr. Viner had gone ahead and made the film, casting Deborah Raffin in the starring role. Happily, Carmen was pleased with the production.

Her fourth screenplay, broadcast during the 1979–1980 season, was a CBS production called *To Race the Wind*. For this she had adapted a book by Harold Krent, which was a personal account of the author's trials and tribulations as a blind student at Harvard. Far from being a melodramatic or ponderous account of blindness, Carmen had found the book very funny. That's what had appealed to her about it. She had never written a comedy before and wanted to try.

When CBS offered her the story about the blind student, she was tempted to turn it down. She was already hard at work on a very ambitious original screenplay called *The Last Days of Pompeii* that NBC had commissioned her to do. After a tremendous amount of research, she had recreated ancient Pompeii just as she felt it had been when nearby Mount Vesuvius erupted, burying the town and its citizenry under tons of volcanic ash. In this historical setting, she had woven a story about a gladiator as the central character. But, after deciding also to take on the adaptation of Harold Krent's book she couldn't immerse herself totally in the story of this gladiator. One day she would be in ancient Pompeii; the next she would have to leap across centuries to be with a blind boy at Harvard. It entailed quite a switch in thinking, this jumping back and forth from historical drama to contemporary comedy. But with deadlines on both screenplays, she had no choice but to keep doing it that way.

By mid-1980, only five years after she had enrolled reluctantly in a screenwriting course, five of Carmen's screenplays had appeared on television as full-length feature films. On the surface there seems little about any one of the stories that bears much resemblance to the others. But Carmen sees a common thread that runs through almost all of them.

"I find I'm particularly interested in looking at people who are going through some process of change. In other words, people who are presented with a challenge and who, in dealing with that challenge, find that they are making fundamental changes in their lives. It happens that I have usually written about women who are in this process of struggling. Willa; the Betty Rollin character; and Teeny, the mother who abused, all make fundamental life changes as a result of challenge. And, of course, so does Mary, the mother of Jesus."

As a woman writer, Carmen feels strongly that one of the biggest contributions she can make is, simply to write about other women accurately. "Even a cursory look at movies of the past indicates that women are poorly understood. They tend to do and say what men think they should do and say, but rarely—in my opinion—what real women would do and say. I think women often approach life quite differently from men; and so I find myself in the gratifying position of letting the world in on that. Television is so powerful in its influence on our lives. ¶It is important to me that I have the opportunity of portraying women as real, full-blown human beings."

She is proud of the women she has created. Within the television industry, she has had to fight for each one of them. "*Every* female character I have ever written has been criticized as too strong. 'Better *soften* her,' they say. For which, read, 'Make her more like the cardboard cutouts we've always had — a little dumb, very dependent, nonthreatening.'"

Carmen's criticism of television goes beyond sexism. "There's a failure of the imagination at work in television, a willingness to sacrifice good stuff for a car crash, a need to sacrifice the whole effort to get those ratings. It is a state of mind, the collective network mentality that you can't offend anyone — and for 'offend' read 'make them think, or question.' Lurking at the bottom of all this is a not-so-secret conviction that the audience is not very smart."

Still, on balance, Carmen feels that the rewards of writing for television far outweigh the frustrations. What other medium, she asks, offers the opportunity to speak to millions of people, to move them, to help them understand something about their lives? Besides that, "It's just plain fun," she says. "It's exciting to be involved in a creative endeavor. As a screenwriter, you have the opportunity to make more money than most of the highest-paid executives in the nation — male or female — and you can do it with relatively few strings. You need only yourself, some paper, and a typewriter."

Sound easy? And glamorous? Well, it's not *that* easy, according to Carmen. "Yes, I have glamorous lunches with glamorous people, but I don't do it every day. I write. To be a successful screenwriter, you need more than just talent. You need an enormous amount of self-discipline and stamina."

Her own discipline begins at eight-thirty every morning when she sits down to begin writing. She keeps writing until three in the afternoon when the twins arrive home from school. If she is working under more pressure than usual, she will continue writing at night and on Saturdays as well. On the average, it takes her three months to write an original screenplay, including doing the research, plotting the story, and writing it.

Carmen feels it would be extremely difficult for an unknown

writer to become a successful screenwriter without living on the West Coast. Los Angeles has always been the center of the motion picture industry, the place where actors, writers, directors, and producers congregate. Throughout the 1950's, however, television entertainment was produced live out of New York by the networks and their advertisers. With production costs climbing and the networks becoming more sophisticated in methods of getting the best value for their dollar, television entertainment turned to film and moved west. These days, all prime-time television entertainment originates in southern California. The networks do not produce their own shows; they hire independent producers to do that. Nonetheless, the ultimate decision about how American television viewers will be entertained nightly comes from CBS's headquarters in Studio City, from NBC in Burbank, and ABC in Century City.

In this film world of southern California, no one works in a vacuum. Having contacts and knowing other people in the industry are essential. Producers go back to actors, writers, and directors that they've worked well with in the past. Television executives tend to listen to writers who come recommended by favorite producers. To establish these all-important contacts, a young writer with no film credits must often be willing to be bold to the point of brashness. Hollywood is not for the timid of heart.

In her own early days as a writer, Carmen remembers driving down Sunset Boulevard in Beverly Hills. Stopping for a traffic light, she glanced around and spotted the well-known screenwriter Paul Schraeder sitting in a booth in a coffee shop having his morning coffee. Right then and there, Carmen parked her car, went into the shop, introduced herself, and plopped down across from him. "He couldn't have been nicer," she remembers. "I asked him dozens of questions about screenwriting and we talked for a long time. These days, writers who are just starting out do the same thing to me."

Since her success, certain aspects of Carmen's professional life have changed. Not only does she make a great deal more money, but she no longer writes anything without being paid first. Nor does she have to go through the step-by-step process of having each stage of a screenplay approved before being told to go to the next stage. Now when she is hired to write something, her agent asks for and gets her full fee up front, before anyone knows whether her screenplay will ever be produced or not.

In contrast to her professional life, her private life has changed very little. Calvin has enjoyed the same measure of success in his new business that she's had in hers. In spite of their vastly improved financial situation, the Culvers remain in their same house in Encino, having chosen to renovate it rather than to move into the prohibitive real estate market of nearby Beverly Hills. From this house, where Carmen does all of her writing, she constantly struggles to find some sort of balance between the demands of her career and those of raising young children.

"I'm afraid I handle it all very badly, and with constant angst," she despairs. "I live in a perpetual state of unfinished tasks and self-recriminations about whether or not I'm neglecting my children. In fact, there are no easy ways to work and have a pulled-together home life. My husband does his fair share and, if he didn't, life would be impossible."

Despite the pressures, Carmen has never been happier. She loves her work, a fact that has positive effects on her personal life. She sees her life now as having taken on a wholeness that was not there when she was younger. Without any one of the interlocking pieces—her work, her children, her marriage, her ability to put aside her writing and spend two weeks making bedspreads for her daughters' beds—there would be no whole.

"I never wrote until I had children. To tell the truth, I don't think I had nearly as much to write about. Having a family, having these various relationships as wife and mother has given me perspectives which I lacked before. So whereas having children is supposed to doom women professionally, I have found the opposite to be true."

She hesitates then . . . "It sounds like Pollyanna, but here it is: When I had the children, I suddenly wasn't afraid of anything any more. All the reasons I had found not to write suddenly disappeared."

Betty Rollin, best-selling author and NBC news correspondent. *(Photo courtesy NBC News, New York)*

CHAPTER 5

BETTY ROLLIN

□ NATIONAL NEWS CORRESPONDENT AND AUTHOR □

"STANDING BY . . ."

Inside a sound-proof television studio deep within New York's Rockefeller Center complex, NBC has begun taping the second in a series of three news specials. Titled *Women Like Us,* the series, is for women and it is about women. It is an attempt to deal seriously and intelligently with the everyday concerns and dilemmas that women share with each other.

"Tape getting up to speed . . . " a male voice announces from the rear of the studio.

Not a murmur is heard from the largely female studio audience. Ten days from now when the show will be aired for an early afternoon national audience, it will last only an hour. The studio audience, here to participate in the show, knows that today's taping will take at least three hours. They are eager for it to begin.

"Waiting for tape . . . "

The hush continues. All eyes are on the glamorous brunette, dressed in a delicate shade of peach, who stands center stage soberly staring into the camera. It is Betty Rollin, familiar to millions as a veteran correspondent on NBC's national *"Nightly News."* She is the anchorwoman for the series.

"We are up to speed . . . "

Still very serious, apparently unconscious of anything but the camera and the director, Betty gives an exaggerated yawn, stretching her face muscles for one last time. Suddenly the expression comes fully and dazzlingly alive. She begins speaking, enunciating every syllable of her carefully written opening in a clear, earnest voice. Her manner conveys such intimacy and warmth that it's as if she were reaching out and touching every last one of the people in her vast television audience, opening the front door of her own home and inviting them in.

The taping is off to a good start. The studio audience visibly relaxes. Clearly the show is in the hands of a pro — a woman so smart, self-confident, and facile that it's as if she's been born to occupy this stage. And therein lies the irony. Not a single woman watching her from the studio audience can quite believe that Betty Rollin is just another run-of-the-mill woman, a woman, as the title suggests, *like us.*

The private Betty Rollin, however, is quite another person from the public one. Far from being immune to the problems other women face, she has battled cancer, had a breast removed, weathered the break-up of a marriage, and is still somewhat bothered by her decision to have no children. Far from being born to occupy center stage, she says, "I never had any goals. If I'd had goals, I would have been nowhere."

In attitude and in fact, Betty is the quintessential New Yorker. Born in the city in 1936 and raised in the nearby suburbs of Yonkers and Bronxville, she has spent all of her adult life living in one of Manhattan's most thickly populated midtown neighborhoods. There is nothing the slightest bit wide-eyed about Betty. She is sophisticated, savvy, witty, pleased with her success, but frequently irreverent about herself. When asked whether it isn't a marvelously heady thing to be a star of network news, she merely shrugs. "Not particularly," she says. "I don't need to have my face on TV. There are two sides to television, show business and jouralism. I am a journalist. That's my value to the network."

Betty may not have had specific goals when she was growing up, but she always knew that one day she would work. As an only child, doted upon by two adoring parents, she says of herself, "In a sense, I was both a son and a daughter — the prince and the princess. Like a daughter, I was expected to get married and have children. Like a son, I was expected to have a job and do something. My parents wanted everything for me."

Although Mrs. Rollin gave up teaching to be a full-time mother to her only child, there was always an aura of professionalism about her. She was bright, capable, and energetic, a woman who could have chosen to do just about anything. Avidly interested in all things cultural, she saw to it that Betty took piano and dancing and dramatic lessons. Says Betty, "My mother was devoted to the idea of educating me, seeing that I got somewhere. Not that she wanted me to be president or anything like that. She never talked in terms of my having a specific profession or in terms of financial success. It's funny; although I've done very well financially, I've never pursued money. I've always gone after the things I wanted to do."

Although Betty was caught up in a whirlwind of activity outside her home, an entirely different atmosphere existed within the Rollin household. There it was calm and unhurried, a good balance for the other side of her life. "I spent most of my time drawing and reading and drawing and reading. I loved being sick because that meant more time to draw and read."

In eighth grade Betty went off to the Fieldston Ethical Culture School, a very expensive private school located within the northernmost boundary of New York City. Although Fieldston was considerably less than a half-hour's drive from her home, it might have been a million miles away, so different were its students from the girls and boys she'd grown up with in public school.

Largely from sophisticated urban neighborhoods, these new classmates were both street-smart and book-smart, far more absorbed by their education than her earlier group of friends. Intellectually inquisitive and competitive with each other, they were constantly challenging the status quo, always looking for answers other than those in their text books. Betty was awed and delighted by her new city-bred friends. As the years passed and it came time for her to consider college, she wanted a place as intellectually exciting as Fieldston. She didn't have to look far. She chose Sarah Lawrence College, located in Bronxville.

"Sarah Lawrence was Fieldston carried one step further. The first thing I remember feeling when I got there was thank goodness I'd had my ears pierced when I was younger. As far as dressing well or wearing lipstick, that was out of the question!"

Traditionally Sarah Lawrence women have always prided themselves on being different from more conventional college women. In the mid-1950's an attitude of bohemianism prevailed on campus. The emphasis was on experimentation—academically, artistically, and in one's personal life. At home, however, Betty was getting the opposite message. Her parents were firm believers in the old-fashioned values, and they weren't about to tolerate much deviation on the part of their daughter. Feeling torn between the dictates of her parents and those of her college friends, Betty often felt as though she were balanced on a tightrope between the two. "It was a rather difficult period for me. Still, I loved Sarah Lawrence. To this day, all the most original women I know came from there."

Because Sarah Lawrence allowed its students a great deal of flexibility and independence in their course selections, Betty spent four years taking only subjects that appealed to her. In retrospect, she feels this is why she didn't get the best education. "I never took a single math, science, language, or even history course. It wasn't required. But I would have been far better off if I had."

She continues. "Nowadays, I meet a lot of kids who want careers in television. So off they go to places that give them courses called Communications I or Communications II. What does that mean? I've never been able to figure it out, except that I suppose it gives them some of the technical training. Well, you don't need that. You learn that quickly enough. What you do need is a good, well-rounded education with lots and lots of reading on the side."

Midway through college an English teacher made a startling comment to Betty. Complimenting her on the natural way she seemed to be able to express herself on paper, he suggested that she consider becoming a professional writer. Betty didn't take the suggestion seriously. "I certainly didn't think I could be a writer. I didn't think I was smart enough." Besides, by now she was becoming increasingly involved in the theater department, even toying with the idea of becoming an actress. "I didn't want to be a Hollywood star. The *the-ah-tah* was what interested me," she says melodramatically. "My ideal was Katherine Cornell, not Marilyn Monroe."

But even the theater was more of a fantasy than a concrete goal. Then, merely by chance, a New York theater agent spotted her in a college play during the spring of her senior year. Suddenly, without ever having made a firm commitment to a career on the stage, she had a small part in an off-Broadway production of *The Country Wife*, starring Frances Sternhagen.

It all seemed so easy. Here she was attending her own graduation and starting rehearsals for a New York play all in the same day! Had anybody ever led a life so charmed? Overnight she had become a promising young professional actress with no place to go but up. When *The Country Wife* ended, she made the rounds of auditions and threw herself into acting classes, studying with Sanford Mizener, one of the all-time great acting coaches. "That was good work with Mizener, and it helped me later on," she says. "The premise of his classes was based on being direct and truthful, not fudging around but finding imaginative ways to express oneself without being trite."

Among the thousands of young men and women who flock to New York with dreams of a life in the theater, Betty was one of the lucky ones. By living in a series of cheap sublet apartments, she managed, just barely, to support herself. Still, the life was hard, often extremely painful. For every successful audition, there were dozens of shattering rejections, each one punishing the psyche and sapping away at self-confidence. In 1961, nearly five years after graduating from college, she was called out to California to make a pilot for a television series. "Thank goodness it didn't sell! Otherwise, I still might be in that life," she says with deep disgust.

Forced to look for ways to support herself, she had an idea for a book. "Actually," she explains, "it was a nonbook, a collection of marriage vows that I got someone to illustrate." Without including a word of her own writing, she sold the book, *I Thee Wed*, to Doubleday and Company. To her surprise, it did very well.

Her editor wanted more book ideas. This time he urged her to include some of her own writing. It was silly for her to think she couldn't do it, he said. From what he'd seen, he felt she had a very appealing and natural way of expressing herself. Betty was skeptical. True, writing came easily to her, but that was the trouble. Whoever said that writing was *supposed* to be all that easy? Nonetheless, she agreed to try. Her second nonbook, written partly in her own words, was called *Mothers Are Funnier than Children*. It, too, was a success.

She got a little bolder. Buying up dozens of magazines, she took them home and studied the articles in each, noting the type of reader to which each magazine was addressed as well as the content, style, and tone of the articles. Finally, she felt ready to begin writing. It wasn't long before she had sold her first magazine article to *McCalls*.

That did it. Writing *was* easy, she decided. Moreover, she loved it — so much so that she gave up all thoughts of remaining in the theater. Hearing that Joan Didion was resigning as associate features editor at *Vogue* magazine, Betty decided to apply. With nothing but two little nonbooks and one magazine article to her credit, she knew she really wasn't qualified. Drawing on every bit of her training as an actress, she succeeded in talking her way in.

Because *Vogue* was primarily a fashion magazine, bought for its dazzling display of the latest fashions, its feature articles didn't have to be commercial. Not only was there a great deal of freedom in content but always an insistence upon high literary quality. "It was the best writing experience I've ever had," says Betty. "I worked under Allene Talmey, who was a great writing teacher because she was such a tough editor. Being at *Vogue* was like being at military school. I've never worked so hard in my life."

From *Vogue,* less than a year later, Betty went over to *Look* magazine. By now she had published a few more magazine articles and *Look* regarded her as a highly competent freelance writer with lots of good ideas. One of the top editors at *Look,* Pat Carbine, particularly liked her work. Within a short time, Betty was no longer a freelance. She was a senior editor with her own columns prominently featured every few weeks.

During the six years she remained at *Look,* Betty became known through her columns to people all over the country. To thousands of unseen faces, she was a helpless, urban friend, a woman who made them feel a little better about themselves because of her own willingness to divulge so much about herself. Nothing seemed quite so absurd as to find that Betty Rollin had been sent to write a story about the football players on the Los Angeles Rams, especially when she began her article by confessing, "There are three things I really hate: good music, sports, and the outdoors."

Says Betty, "When you write a column you become a kind of persona. It's not that the character isn't you, because it is a part of you. It's just that you take it to the nth degree to achieve a tone that is a little helpless and a little arch. The trick in doing it is to avoid being cute."

Betty did not confine herself to light-hearted subjects. Her article, "The Motherhood Myth" was a serious and, at the time, rather radical essay that questioned the idea of motherhood for all women. Why was there this enormous pressure on women to bear children? she asked. Why did Mrs. X feel she was any less of a woman than Mrs. Y simply because Mrs. Y had children and Mrs. X did not? These questions, and Betty's conclusions, drew more mail than any other article in the history of *Look.* Later it was published in college text books and translated into several languages.

"The article came out of questions I was asking myself at the time. I've never had the intense need for children that other women express. Also, I knew I couldn't be the kind of mother that my mother had been to me because I didn't want to give up working. And yet I didn't want to be any less of a mother than my mother had been."

Today, more than a decade after writing the article, she says, "I don't think it's wonderful I didn't have children. I think I've missed something, no question about it. On the other hand, that's what I chose and that's how it worked out. I think the decision was right for me."

In 1971 *Look* went out of business. The only other magazine similar to it was *Life*, but Betty had heard that it, too, was having financial problems. Not wanting to work for a woman's magazine or an all-news magazine, she began wondering about the possibilities of being a journalist for television. "I had no idea what I was in for! I just thought that television journalism was a different kind of journalism. It didn't occur to me that the major job of a TV reporter or correspondent is producing film."

She auditioned for NBC and was hired. Not only was she seen as a journalist with an impressive background, but even more important, she was a woman. In 1971 NBC and the other networks were beginning to realize that, like it or not, they had to seek out qualified women.

Betty started as an associate producer for "First Tuesday," a monthly news documentary with a magazine format. Although she knew next to nothing about the technical side of television, she felt good about the things she could do. Since each show consisted of several stories (like a magazine), she used a number of ideas she'd had as a print journalist for these filmed stories. People were nice to her. From top management on down, they knew of her background as a national columnist. They tended to make allowance for whatever she didn't know about television.

Also during that first year she was made drama critic for WNBC-TV, the local NBC station. Covering openings of plays and musicals on and off Broadway was fun, but it was also arduous work. Because she had to be back at the station in time to give her critique on the eleven-o'clock news, there was little time for rewriting and polishing her reports. To New York viewers, however, it was clear from the start that she had a quality not often seen on television. Though she spoke with simplicity, her style was unusually eloquent. Obviously this was a woman who cared a great deal about language.

Having been an actress, Betty knew how to project herself on

On her way to a news assignment, Betty hurriedly freshens up for her on-camera appearance. *(Photo credit: Susan Wood)*

television. People being trained for on-camera jobs in television news never are given voice and speech lessons. "It would be a good idea if they were," says Betty. "There are a lot of print journalists who could be very fine television journalists if they had a little of that training."

Exactly one year after coming to NBC, Betty was asked to become a network correspondent reporting on national news. "I practically didn't know what a correspondent was," she says. She agreed to spend the next few months being trained for the job at the local NBC station.

No longer was she the new arrival from *Look*. She had been in television for a year, and over at the local station people either ignored or forgot about her background. The only thing they did know was that she was a woman in her mid-thirties who knew appallingly little about television news.

"It was a humiliating period for me. I felt very small, utterly unimportant, and very, very junior. Also, I hated all that running around following people on local stories. What am I doing? Why am I here? I kept asking myself."

Yet out of the humiliation came an absolute determination to prove herself. Because she'd always found criticism helpful, one day she went up to her boss, the man in charge of local news. "You know," she said, "I'm kind of new at this. So if you have anything critical to say about me, I'd appreciate hearing it."

"Well," he replied, "I don't like anything you do."

Betty was stunned. Recovering, she asked, "Okay, but why?"

"I'll have to think about it and let you know."

Days passed, then a couple of weeks. The man never mentioned the subject. Finally Betty asked again.

"Oh," he said, "I guess I just don't like women on the air. Unless they're *really* good looking, of course, like Pia Lindstrom [local WNBC-TV reporter]."

Says Betty. "Nobody should have to take that kind of abuse from another person. The worst of it is you can't get angry because that's your boss. So you wait till you get home and then you get angry."

In January, 1973, Betty was named a full-fledged NBC news correspondent. Assigned to the northeastern bureau, she was the only woman and the only New Yorker on a staff that included a bureau chief, four other correspondents, three field producers, and a news director. Instantly she felt the enormous difference between network news and local news. Not only were the stories on network far more interesting, but the stress was on good, serious journalism. Whereas a show business quality had existed in local news, with lots of light-hearted banter that emphasized the sparkling personalities of reporters and anchors, the correspondents on national news were not supposed to be personalities. They were journalists; their job was to get the story and report it in a clear, straightforward way.

It was exciting work. She covered an all-night prison riot in West Virginia, the trials of several nationally known figures, the murder of Governor Sharples of Bermuda. These headline-making stories, involving spot reporting and nonembellishment of fact, interested her more as life experiences, however, than they did as journalistic experiences. What intrigued her as a journalist were stories much like the ones she'd done for *Look*. Not the immediate news, not the headlines of the day, but in-depth interviews with interesting people and behind-the-scene reports on how people lived and coped with their problems.

Increasingly she was assigned this type of story. Some of them were interviews or reports presented as part of the day's news. But

Surrounded by cameraman, crew, and field producer, Betty waits to go on-camera. *(Photo credit: Susan Wood)*

others, particularly in later years, were developed into longer stories and presented on two or three consecutive evenings as the final "Segment III" section of the news. Because these longer stories were like mini-documentaries, Betty often spent nearly a month on each. Not only did she do all her own writing and rewriting but she also did much of the research, advised on the filming, and spent hours in the editing room. Among her most memorable reports were 'Women at Work,' a study of why women are increasingly working outside the home; 'The Children Nobody Wants,' a report on the family foster-care program, and 'His, Hers, and Theirs,' a story about family life in second marriages.

"I'm one of the few women in network news — in fact, I may be the only one — who would be caught dead doing women's subjects," says Betty. "Women who come into this business only want to do what is called "hard news," the headline-breaking news of the day. They are hell-bent and determined to do what the men have done. Maybe because I'm older and had proved myself in another field I've never felt I had to prove myself by covering war, pestilence, and famine."

She goes on. "The things I do on TV are always called "soft news" or "soft subjects." Well, I resent that description, but I ignore it. I don't think a story about foster-care children is any softer than holding a microphone up to a politician's face. If he's lying, he knows he's lying and you know he's lying, and he knows you know he's lying. That's *hard* news? Well, I'm sorry, but I don't find that interesting work."

In 1974 the news of Betty Ford's breast cancer was "hard" news. It was "hard" news because Betty Ford was the wife of the president and that made it headlines. Correspondents on all three networks told the nation that the First Lady had undergone a mastectomy, a standard surgical procedure removing her cancerous breast.

On September 30, 1974, Betty Rollin stood before a nationwide audience and did a follow-up story on the country's reaction to Betty Ford's mastectomy. She and a camera crew had gone to a cancer detection center in New York, the Guttman Breast Diagnostic Institute. On camera, Betty said, "The terror that women feel about breast cancer is not unreasonable. What is unreasonable is that women still turn inward. They think if they avoid investigating the possibility that they have the disease, they'll avoid the disease. But as cases of such prominent women as Betty Ford become known, other women are turning their fear into the kind of action that can save lives."

It was a "soft" news story, the type of story that Betty liked to do and did well. Not only had it involved some thorough research on her part and good solid reporting of facts, but it had confronted a deep, unspoken fear that women have and turned it into something positive. She had been able to let women know that they weren't helpless victims. She'd given them specific ways to detect breast cancer in themselves before it was too late.

Six months later Betty lay in a hospital bed in New York recovering from her own mastectomy. When she'd given her report from the Guttman Institute, she'd known far more about breast cancer than most people. What she didn't know was that even as she spoke to the nation she had it, too.

Nothing in her experience as a woman or as a journalist could have prepared her for this. It was a devastating blow. She felt ugly. Worse, she was terrified. She had lost a breast, but had they gotten all the cancer? No matter what they said, she couldn't be sure. Almost as if she saw herself as an entirely different person than she'd

In a sound-proof booth, Betty records her day's story. *(Photo credit: Susan Wood)*

been before, she began scrutinizing every aspect of her former life. Three years earlier she'd gotten married for the first time to a writer named Arthur Herzog. At times the marriage had seemed shaky. Now she began considering the possibility of divorce. She went back to her job at NBC eight days after arriving home from the hospital. It didn't work. She couldn't concentrate. Finally, after asking for a leave of absence from the network, she left her husband, left New York, and went to live with a friend in another city.

Already she had begun to write. It was a natural response, an instinct so basic that she couldn't have done otherwise. Telling the story of her mastectomy was a way of unraveling her own confusion, a way of dealing with the pain. What began as a few thoughts written for herself one morning a few weeks after the operation led her on and on. Nine months after her surgery she had completed a book. She called it *First, You Cry.*

"When I started writing, I didn't think I'd wind up telling as much as I told. But there was no way else to do it and be honest." Indeed, she *was* honest. Seldom had any woman described so intimate an experience with such candor. It was a brave, touching account, told with a good deal of self-deprecating humor and without even a trace of self-pity. Immediately it became a best-seller. Far more important than the book's success, however, was what had happened to her. By taking the risk of stripping herself bare for others, a considerable risk for someone so visible to the public, she had worked herself out of her own confusion and unhappiness. At last she felt ready to live fully again.

But not ready to live in quite the same way she had before. That was impossible. She had had cancer; she lived with the fear of its recurrence. As she says in her book, "When the possibility of death is on one's mind, the problems of life, no matter how great or niggling, loom less large. When things go well nowadays, I feel as happy as I ever felt before the operation. But the converse has altered remarkably. When things go badly, I definitely suffer less. A personal hurt, a screw-up at work—such things bother me less now, much less."

And she goes on. "My raised consciousness about death has somewhat raised my consciousness about life. There is, I find, a recurring jingle in my head:

> Am I doing
> what I'd want to be doing
> if I were dying?"

Five years later as she sits in her office at NBC talking to a visitor, it is clear that the answer to that question is a resounding yes. "It sounds strange," she says, "but I'm kind of grateful for the cancer experience, assuming that it's over, which, I guess, is an assumption I can't make. I think anyone who's had cancer is afraid for the rest of his or her life. Every time I get a cold practically I'm tense about it. But that's okay. I can live with that. And, in a sense, that's how we all should live. All I know is that I'm much happier now than I ever was before."

A great deal has happened since she finished her book. Although her first marriage ended in divorce, she has remarried. Her new husband, Harold Edwards, is a professor of mathematics and as handsome as any movie star. Betty beams when she talks about him. "He's incredible! He has no faults, at least none that I can see." Then, undoubtedly remembering that she's a journalist and not supposed to exaggerate the truth, she hesitates for a moment, as if wracking her brain for at least one tiny fault. "No," she adds, "he *really* has no faults. He's brilliant, for one thing, and he's kind, sensitive, thoughtful and . . . well, he loves *me*." She flashes a dazzling smile, as if not quite believing the miracle of it all.

In addition to her new marriage, she has seen the story of her ordeal with breast cancer retold as a two-hour television feature film. With Mary Tyler Moore playing her and Anthony Perkins as her first husband, Arthur, she watched as all the extraordinarily personal details of her real-life drama unfolded before an audience of millions. "It was a weird feeling, really bizarre," she admits. Happily, she had only one minor criticism of the television production: "Hollywood gave us a dining room. Such a hoot—as if we ever had a dining room!"

Although Betty had nothing to do with the television version and only visited the set one day, it was impossible to distance herself from the filming altogether. Outside the NBC building at Rockefeller Center, the director and camera crew were busily filming Mary Tyler Moore re-creating the hectic life of a national news correspondent. Inside the NBC building, Betty was hard at work being that correspondent.

But not quite the same correspondent that she'd been before. True, the pace was as fast as it ever was. She was constantly packing and repacking her suitcase, dashing off to planes, tearing around to locations everywhere in the country. Since cancer, however, she'd been even more insistent upon doing the kind of journalism that she does best, fully developed stories that would provoke viewers into dealing with a whole range of issues and ideas that go beyond the headlines.

One such story was a three-part Segment III report on dying. In it she told about the recent emphasis on making death less frightening for dying patients and their families. It was a tough assignment, one that she worked on for a month. Having had cancer, it was impossible to feel journalistically detached when she interviewed dozens of terminally ill patients in their hospital beds. "One of the pieces in the story disturbed me so much that I couldn't stand to watch it. I couldn't sleep nights just thinking about it," she says. Still, she's proud of the story mostly because, again, she was able to take an unspeakably sad subject, confront it honestly, and turn it into something positive.

As NBC News began the decade of the 1980's, there was a change of management that resulted in some changes of their news presentation. "Nowadays," says Betty, "you'd never find a story on dying on the Nightly News. It would be considered too soft." Thus Betty moved into doing more documentaries. In January, 1979, she cohosted a three-hour prime-time "NBC News Special" called 'The American Family—an Endangered Species?'. She's also hosted a one-hour "NBC Reports" on learning disabilities and how they relate to delinquent behavior in young people.

She felt good about her afternoon series, "Women Like Us." Unlike the old daytime women's shows that often featured celebrities giggling and gossiping in a kaffee-klatch setting, Betty's show was woven around a single, serious topic that was explored through film strips and lively, intelligent conversation. "NBC wanted a series of daytime shows for women," she explains. "So I created the concept and thought up the title." She had reason to be pleased. The series got excellent ratings. As she had thought, there are a lot of women watching afternoon television who crave intelligent programming.

The summer of 1980 brought Betty some exciting news. Earlier in the year, while anchoring the "Women Like Us" series, she had been thinking more and more about an idea for a book. Since graduating from college, she had been closely involved in three exciting professional worlds—the world of the New York theater, the world of magazine publishing, the world of television. She wanted to write about them, tracing her own, personal experiences as a young actress, a magazine writer, and a TV journalist. On the basis of a brief summary and roughly thirty pages of sample chapters, her not-yet-written book was presented to several leading book publishers. There was interest—a lot of it. So much so, in fact, that a two-day auction took place with several publishers bidding against each other for the right to publish it. Finally it was sold to Little-Brown for an undisclosed but reputedly very sizable sum of money.

Thus, as this book goes to press, Betty has again taken a leave of absence from NBC to spend full time writing her book. Upon its completion she hopes and expects to return to television, doing the kind of in-depth journalism that she's been doing right along. "I'm ambitious," she says, "but if being important in television means doing what I don't want to do, then I don't want to be that important. It's true, I'll never cover a political convention and I'll never be a news anchor, but I don't care. Anchoring the news, frankly, is the most boring job there is."

Although television has never yet featured a gray-haired woman—the counterpart of a Walter Cronkite—in any on-camera news job, Betty refuses to worry about what will happen to her TV career as she grows older. Having battled cancer, she has developed a perspective on her life that reduces such what-if questions to total insignificance. "I think I'll look okay in my fifties," she says. "And if I don't? Well, that's okay, too. I'll produce, or I'll write."

To Betty Rollin, highly successful author and television correspondent, the future is clearly full of options.

CHAPTER 6

RISA KORRIS

□ CAMERAWOMAN □

BEHIND A LONG RECTANGULAR TABLE on stage in a college auditorium sits a panel of experts. They are leading a weekend symposium on the growing international problem of chemical wastes. CBS Television feels its viewers ought to be aware of this dangerous form of pollution and has sent a producer and camera crew to cover the discussion. For CBS this is the beginning of filming that will take place around the world, the first step in what is hoped will end with another hour-long, hard-hitting documentary in the series, "CBS Reports."

The crew, stationed at one side of the stage, is the basic, minimum-sized crew used for documentaries. There is a cameraman, an assistant cameraman, a lighting man, and a sound man. Today, however, the term camera*man* is a misnomer. Operating the highly complex Aaton television camera is Risa Korris, a slender young woman whose long brown hair tumbles over her face as she bends her five-foot-nine-inch frame only slightly to peer through the lens.

Risa is the only female member of today's crew. But that's not unusual. In the television industry, where so much depends upon the camera, Risa is one of only a handful of camerawomen deemed experienced and skilled enough to be consistently hired for what is still widely considered the job of a man.

Risa works quietly and unobtrusively. Because today's shooting involves an indoor, stationary setting, she is the only one of the crew to do much moving about. With her camera perched on its heavy steel tripod, she focuses on the panel. Briefly she consults with the assistant cameraman whose job it is to load the film and make sure it's

Camerawoman Risa Korris.

dust-free. When it's time for questions from the audience, she un-snaps the camera from the tripod and carries it to the rear of the stage for a better angle. She moves with exquisite grace. So easily does she handle the more than twenty-pound weight of the camera that it's as if it were part of her own body.

Halfway through the morning, the panel takes a break. As the crew mills about on stage, a teenage girl shyly approaches Risa. "All I want to say is that . . . well, that I've never seen a camera*woman* before and I think you're wonderful!"

Quietly, Risa thanks the girl — so quietly that it's as if she's hoping no one else overheard. Clearly she's sensitive to being singled out merely for being a woman. On her own biographical resume, she carefully avoids drawing attention to her sex. She calls herself a cameraman.

As a child, Risa saw no great difference between what men and women were capable of doing with their lives. Born in 1946, she grew up in a family where all the adults worked, even her grandmother. Risa's father, David Korris, was a dentist—"a fabulous dentist," according to Risa, who commuted from home in Jamaica Estates, Long Island, to an office in nearby Manhattan. Her mother, Roma Korris, was a piano teacher and accompanist who later became the head of her own small textile firm. Besides Risa there was also her younger brother, Jim.

"We were a very close family; we still are," says Risa. With her parents as examples, she adds, she simply took it for granted that one day her life, too, would include a job. "I always thought that I was going to be a painter—another Georgia O'Keefe. It was a very strange feeling to go through my life so convinced of what I wanted to do, and then have it turn out so differently."

Recognizing their young daughter's obvious need to express herself creatively, Mr. and Mrs. Korris encouraged her to explore. Risa not only took art lessons, but she also studied music and dance. As time passed, it became even clearer that she was an extremely talented artist, but that wasn't all. Small-boned and willowy, she had also developed into an extraordinarily graceful young ballerina, so gifted, in fact, as to be considered promising material for the professional stage. With her mother's encouragement, Risa auditioned for both the American Ballet Theatre and the Metropolitan Opera Company. As a result, she was invited to join the classes for young people being trained for the ballet corps at the opera.

By high school Risa was spending two afternoons a week at dance classes in New York City as well as taking art classes at either the city's Museum of Modern Art or the Art Students League. Commuting was time consuming. In her sophomore year, she transferred from her public school in Long Island to the Dalton School, a private school in the City. Even though it meant that her mother had to drive her into New York each morning, it seemed worth the trouble. Dalton was known as one of the finest schools in the country. Famous for its open-ended, progressive approach to education, which put a special emphasis on nurturing the individuality and unique talents of each of its students, it seemed the perfect place for Risa.

At Dalton Risa continued her art classes at the Metropolitan Museum. By now there was no lingering doubt about her future career. She gave up ballet to spend even more time on her painting. A few months before graduation, she got some exciting news. On the basis of a portfolio of art she'd submitted, she was accepted into the University of Pennsylvania's Graduate School of Art. For a high school senior it was a most unusual situation. She would be entering college as a freshman, taking all the standard courses that all freshman take, except for art. There she'd be over in the graduate school—by far the best graduate school of art, she felt, in the entire country. She couldn't wait to get to college the following September!

Only a few days after arriving in Philadelphia, however, all the excitement and anticipation she'd felt turned into despair. There had been a mistake, the dean told her. Under no circumstances could an undergraduate take graduate courses. As far as the dean was concerned the matter was closed.

"I should have fought the decision," says Risa, still rather bitter about the incident. "Instead, I went along with it and, as a result, my painting suffered tremendously. The undergraduate art department couldn't compare to what I would have gotten in the graduate school."

Although she majored in art history and painting, Risa felt that she made little artistic progress during her four years in college. As graduation neared, she wondered about what to do next, how she would support herself. "I thought about going on to art graduate school, but I felt what they were teaching was too forced, too conceptual for me. I also knew that making a living as an artist is rough."

By now it was 1967, spring of her senior year. Back in New York, her younger brother, Jim, was talking excitedly about the film courses he was taking at high school. Although Risa was totally disinterested in film, she perked up one day when Jim told her that his teacher needed some art work done for a film he was making.

Thinking she might be able to make some extra money, Risa went to see the teacher. It turned out that there had been a misunderstanding. No art was needed. But she and the teacher began talking. Risa told him that following graduation she wanted a job related to art, something in the practical world in which she could make a living.

Why not consider film school? the teacher suggested. As an artist, he said, she couldn't have a better background. Then he described the film program at Columbia University's Graduate

School of the Arts where he'd been a student. Located in New York City, it was one of the few film schools in existence at that time.

He was so enthusiastic that Risa decided to look into the possibility. When she learned that Columbia's program would allow her to combine painting with film-making, that settled it. She applied and was accepted. That fall she entered Columbia.

Almost immediately Risa and the other students were told to go out and start shooting film. Instantly, too, Risa loved it. "When I made my first film, I really got hooked. I knew I wanted to be a camerawoman."

Not all of the students in the film program wanted to do the same thing. Some wanted to be directors; others wanted to be cameramen, editors, or lighting and sound experts. Says Risa, "The thing that was so good about it is that we all learned from each other and we learned a little about every aspect of film." Whatever aspect of film-making they chose, however, the goal was the same. They all wanted to be the best; they all wanted to spend their lives making artistically beautiful feature-length films that would be shown in movie theatres across the country. "Since I was in love with the idea of shooting film," adds Risa, "my dream was to be another James Wong Howe."

For her master's thesis, done during the second and final year, Risa created her own short film titled "Sketches of an Afternoon." She was the producer, director, camerawoman, editor, writer, and artist. "It was a pretty, visual film of a couple walking the streets of New York having a wine-and-cheese romance," Risa explains. "I used a lot of my own sketches and then I'd go from them into live action."

The ability to make a good, original film, however, is of little value to someone straight out of film school. Risa sent out dozens of resumés, hoping that someone would hire her either as an apprentice or an assistant camerawoman. The only response she got came from a very small company asking if she would like to try making a short industrial film to be shown on a continuous cartridge inside an exhibition booth. Nobody else wanted to take a chance on a young camerawoman, still so inexperienced that she didn't even belong to a union.

Risa made the industrial film and went on to work regularly for the small company, sometimes shooting film and sometimes editing it. The place was so small, however, that after a few months she knew

Risa with her crew: right—Jim Korris, director; left—Robert Sands, assistant cameraman.

she had to move on if she was ever to advance professionally. On the basis of her first job, she was hired to be an assistant film editor for a slightly larger company that made industrial films and commercials.

It was a big step up. As a full-time editor, now she could join I.A.T.S.E. (International Alliance of Theatrical Stage Employees), the most prestigious union for film and stage crews. Just as actors must be members of Actors Equity in order even to audition for most roles in the professional theater, so must stage and film crews belong to the union. Without union membership, it is almost impossible to get work.

Still Risa was far from doing what she really wanted to do. Instead of working from behind a camera, she was back in the editing room, painstakingly cutting and splicing other people's film. Nor did her situation show any sign of improving. When the company that had hired her went out of business, she got another job as an assistant editor with a similar small production house. There she was made a negative matcher, working with gloves in a tiny, isolated room making clean versions of film from the original negative. Day in and day out—monotonous, meticulous, and lonely work. She kept hoping that her boss would take pity on her, give her something a little more satisfying to do. "Finally," says she, "I figured that he had no intention of moving me out of my negative room. He was quite pleased with my work there. So I left."

In the year and a half since film school, Risa had edited literally miles of film. Moreover, she realized that film editing didn't have to be boring. At the very top level where editors were in charge of full-length feature films, the work was exciting and challenging, often making the difference between a mediocre film and one of enormous artistic quality. But this top level of film editors was very small, perhaps a total of eight people in the whole of New York. One of the best ways of advancing as a film editor, Risa knew, was to get to know a few of the top editors and, hopefully, be hired to work under them.

A month after quitting her job, Risa was hired as an apprentice editor for *Desperate Characters*, directed by Frank Gilroy. No sooner had she taken the job than Dede Allen, one of the best-known editors in New York, called and wanted her to be an assistant editor for *Slaughterhouse Five*, a big-budget feature film being made by Universal Pictures from Kurt Vonnegut's novel. This *was* an opportunity! Even though she spent a good deal of her time during the next few months sweeping the cutting room floor and fetching other people's lunch, she was also learning, and learning from the best. Although she went on to edit another motion picture, *The Effects of Gamma Rays on Man-In-The-Moon Marigolds*, starring Joanne Woodward, it was the work that she did with Dede Allen on *Slaughterhouse Five* that taught her the most.

By now Risa had given up the idea of ever becoming a camerawoman. Clearly she was an editor, a member of I.A.T.S.E.'s Local 771, the local union for film editors. Only in her spare time did she continue shooting film. "Sometimes I'd talk to the cameramen on the films I was editing and I'd show them my stuff. But that was all."

In early 1972 she heard that NBC was looking for an assistant editor to edit the news. She went for an interview. Realizing when she got there that the job wasn't what she wanted, she started to leave. Heading down the long corridor that led to the elevators, she heard a commotion behind her and turned around. A man in a white lab coat and another man dressed in a three-piece business suit were racing to catch up to her.

"Is it true that you can shoot?" the man in the lab coat asked, holding out a camera.

"Yes," said Risa, quite startled. Then she remembered her resume, which listed her as both cameraman and editor.

"We've got a new camera that's just come out," said the man, showing it to her. "Can you test it for us?"

The camera was a CP-16, one of the first, and much lighter in weight than the clunky cameras then being used. Risa agreed to try.

"First," she says, "I went out to have a cup of coffee just to think about it. It was March and there had been a sudden snowstorm. So I did a thing called 'Flowers Bloom in First New York Snowstorm.' I shot it, brought it back to NBC, and then sailed off without speaking to anyone."

Back home she got a call from them. They needed something with more of a story line, they explained. Could she possibly do a second film? Again Risa agreed.

This time she went off to the zoo in Central Park where she filmed children looking at the animals. Returning home with her film, she suddenly felt paralyzed with fear. "I was sitting there with one hundred feet of film, too terrified to go back to NBC because I was sure that none of it had come out. By now I *cared* about what they thought of me."

She phoned her mother. "Being a working woman herself, my mother had always been particularly helpful to me," says Risa. "Whenever I felt discouraged, she started with the premise that I wasn't alone, that it was always harder for a woman." Now Mrs. Korris urged Risa to get back down to NBC immediately.

As a result of that film, NBC hired Risa on a trial basis, sending her out with local news teams to learn all she could about filming live-action stories. It was a scramble — news crews from different networks converging with each other, all trying to be first on the scene of a fast-breaking story. But at last Risa was shooting film rather than editing it. Now, in addition to her membership in I.A.T.S.E.'s Local 771 for film editors, she became a member of I.A.T.S.E.'s Local 644 for cameramen.

No sooner had Risa joined the NBC crew, however, than she got a call from CBS asking her to be an assistant film editor for a network documentary. NBC advised her to take the job. But after she'd already begun editing for CBS they phoned to say that they'd decided she could have a job as a cameraman with them after all. Then, to make matters even more confusing, after Risa had agreed to work for NBC as a cameraman on weekends and as an editor for CBS weekdays, NBC told her that they'd changed their minds again! Either she agree to work for them full time, they said, or she couldn't have the job with them at all. This was too much for Risa. By now she was not only very much involved with the CBS film, but she felt too committed to the other people working on it to just up and leave. She decided to stay as an editor at CBS.

But inter-network news and gossip travels fast. Little time passed before CBS realized that within their documentary division there was a freelance editor, only twenty-five years old, who was also a skilled professional camerawoman. And so one day Risa got a phone call asking if she'd like to work on a trial basis as a cameraman for the "CBS Evening News" with Walter Cronkite. Within two months Risa's trial period was over. She was made a full-fledged staff camerawoman for the national news.

It was an astonishing leap. Having never had a full-time job on the local news and without ever having worked as an assistant cameraman, which is the traditional way to advance, she now had her own crew for the nightly news! But if this seemed surprising, everything about the past few months had seemed so—the incident with the new camera at NBC, the call from CBS, the call-backs from NBC. All this interest in her from two of the three major networks, Risa is the first to admit, was not due entirely to her own genius. The fact was that she was a woman. In the early 1970's affirmative action programs were forcing the networks to seek out and hire qualified women. Risa's break into television was, first, a matter of being professionally qualified. Then, it was a matter of being the right sex at the right time.

There are few jobs as fast-paced or frantic as the job of cameraman on staff of the national news. Networks divide their news teams into regional bureaus, with each one responsible for covering the news in a specific geographical area. The news crews are small—a cameraman, a sound man, and an electrician. Sometimes a reporter or correspondent or producer accompanies the crew, but not always. In Risa's case what had been a fairly orderly life suddenly became totally unpredictable. Mornings began with checking the posted blue sheets at the station for assignments. Even though Risa was part of the Northeastern Bureau, which operated out of New York, chances were good that the day's assignment would be elsewhere than the city. If so, there would be the rush to pick up assigned film equipment, airplane or car rental information, expense money and credit cards. Next, the race to the airport, the flight, the arrival, the counting and collecting of equipment, the trip out to the location. Then the filming, the ride back to the airport, the recounting of equipment, and finally back again to the network at the end of the day, knowing that the same process would be repeated somewhere else the following day.

"It was exhausting, but it was great," says Risa. "Unlike local news, where you have to cover murder and rape stories, we were shooting really interesting stuff. Right away I did so much traveling. Being on staff I could shoot lots of film and do some experimenting without having to worry that I might get fired."

Although she was the only female traveling with an all-male crew, she never felt uncomfortable. "The crew was like a family. It wasn't as if we were freelance, just there for the day. We were all under contract, our salaries fixed by the union. The men were family men, very much involved with their wives and children. They were great to me."

There was another reason for the close bond that existed among the members of the crew, which Risa was too busy to notice in the beginning. Frequently, news crews are treated somewhat disdainfully by others in the television industry. "It's a big problem," says Risa. "Crews are definitely looked upon as blue collar lackies. The general attitude is that you can't possibly be intelligent. There's no loyalty for the technicians, no protection. You're the enemy, a member of the union."

But the men in her crew supported Risa tremendously, which she especially appreciated as a newcomer. "It would have been much easier if I'd been an assistant cameraman first," she says. "In feature films, you start by loading film and hitting the clapsticks. Then you advance to first assistant, where you're the focus-puller and have more responsibility for the camera. Finally, you become a cameraman and get to shoot. If I'd had a chance to do it that way I would have been able to learn from lots of cameramen in the same way I learned about editing from more experienced film editors. The way I did it, I just had to hash my own way. There was no one to ask. It *was* a little frightening."

But nothing builds self-confidence faster than experience, the day-in-and-day-out process of shooting good, usable film. By her second year of working for the "Evening News," Risa was beginning to see her job in less rosy terms than she had at first. "It's rough work. Your life isn't your own," she says. "You are owned by the network, on call to them all the time." One night in particular stands out. She'd been sent to do a story in Baltimore. The shooting had taken longer than expected and when the exhausted crew arrived at the airport for the late-night flight home they found their plane had been delayed. Wearily Risa called her office to say that she and the crew wouldn't be taking off from Baltimore until midnight.

"Oh?" said the voice on the other end. "Well, thanks for calling. And, by the way, your call tomorrow is for six in the morning. Your flight will leave at seven."

Risa continues: "After the break-in at Watergate, I did a lot of stake-outs. I was on the Mitchell–Stans trial for three months, mostly standing out in front of the courthouse waiting for the defendants and their lawyers to appear. That case was typical of stakeouts. You stand there for hours, sometimes in freezing weather. So many news people are there, all pushing and shoving. You know you have to come back with footage at the end of the day or you're in trouble. But with all those people fighting for the same film sometimes even your own strength isn't enough. Then if you do manage to get something, they don't use it. People in foreign bureaus get especially frustrated. Because of the emphasis on domestic news, their films are so seldom used."

The back-breaking work and long hours were only part of the reason that Risa couldn't see spending her life doing only news. Passionate about the craft of filming, she wanted to go on to films involving more sophisticated camera techniques. She wanted more time to work on individual stories rather than the fleeting involvement she had with daily news. Even more important, she was beginning to realize that unless she expanded, she might be forced eventually to give up filming altogether. Videotape, not film, was increasingly becoming the dominant force in the medium of news.

When she had first started working in news, there had been a big difference between cameramen inside television studios and those who went out on location. Studio cameramen, those who actually filmed Walter Cronkite in the studio delivering the news, used tape. Tape produces an instant picture that is sharper, more realistic than film, giving the viewer more a feeling of actually being there. Cameramen on location used film, which was sent to a lab, developed, and edited before being seen. The two groups of cameramen belonged to two entirely different unions.

But by the mid-1970's the networks were increasingly experimenting with the use of videotape on location also. CBS had taken two or three of their best cameramen from each bureau and trained them to use tape. The group had included Risa, who had then been sent to cover the Boston school strike in tape. After that experience, says Risa, "I decided I didn't want to do it. For one thing, it meant carrying the extra weight of a battery, which in those days weighed thirty pounds. Also, if I'd kept on with tape, I would have been more locked into doing the news than ever."

In June, 1975, Risa got the break she was hoping for. The documentary division at CBS asked her to become a full-time staff camerawoman for them. Risa was thrilled. "I'd always looked up to the people who made documentaries," she says. She knew, too, she had to make the move. "In a sense," she adds, "videotape was forcing me out of the news."

CBS had five national crews that did nothing but documentaries. Because the quality of documentaries is better than news, the crews are larger, always consisting of at least four people, including an assistant cameraman, and often more. Unlike the news, these crews could include outside people, freelancers brought in for special projects. The film equipment was also more sophisticated. Now Risa was shooting in double system, rather than single, and using negative film which gives more latitude to what is being filmed. Too, there were better lights and more advanced sound equipment.

Risa was mostly assigned documentaries with a "magazine" format, hour shows broken into three segments of three entirely different stories. This type of documentary had been gaining in popularity, more and more replacing the hour-long documentaries devoted to a single subject. The best-known magazine show at CBS was "60 Minutes," for which Risa began filming almost immediately. In addition, she filmed for "Who's Who," "CBS Reports," "Lamp Unto My Feet," and the lively children's show, "Razzmatazz."

She continued to travel a great deal, only now she wasn't limited to the Northeast. With the crew, she criss-crossed the country, sometimes staying a week or more at any given location. Because documentaries involved more advanced film techniques, there was more equipment. In and out of airports, Risa was responsible for handling and overseeing thirty separate pieces! But once the crew had arrived on location, there was the luxury of time, the chance to get personally involved in a story. "It was great," she says. "We did a segment on teaching your children at home, so we just moved in with this family in Rhode Island. We lived with them for a week."

Too, there were moments of high drama in documentaries, especially in stories involving investigative journalism. Risa recalls one such instance in "60 Minutes." For a segment on the illegal overloading of trucks by cross-country truck drivers, an employee at CBS had managed to get tapes of a trucker boasting about the ingenious ways he padded the weight of his truck in order to be paid more. But when it came time for the CBS reporter Dan Rather to confront the man on film with proof of his crime, the trucker had vanished. Apparently he'd gotten word that CBS was planning to expose the practice, so he'd simply gone underground for a while.

Just as CBS had about given up on the story for lack of concrete evidence, Risa got a phone call from the producer. The trucker had been found, he said, and would be arriving in Rochester, New York, with a moving van in the morning. Hastily assembling a crew, Risa flew to Rochester. Because the trucker had been told that CBS was doing a rather mild story on families that move, he was not only unsuspicious but actually quite pleased about the idea of being seen by millions of television viewers. Then, with the film rolling, Dan Rather stepped forward and confronted him with his crime. And there it was, a moment preserved on film — a man's face as it changed from arrogance to meanness to anger to shock as it dawned on him that there was nothing he could do, that finally he'd been caught. For Risa, who would never quite be able to forget his expression, it was a moment that no poet or journalist or painter could have captured. It could only have been caught by film.

Although she loved filming CBS documentaries, two-and-a-half years after joining the documentary staff she made one of the riskiest decisions of her career. In February, 1978, she resigned her secure staff position to become a freelance camerawoman. "I wanted to expand and diversify," she explains. "I still wanted to do documentaries, but I also wanted the chance to work on commercials and feature films. I also hoped to become more involved in producing,

Risa takes a light reading for a segment to be shot for NBC's "Prime Time Saturday."

seeing film projects through from beginning to end with a hand in every aspect of production."

Two years after leaving the CBS staff, Risa has no regrets about her decision to be independent. CBS, the network she fondly calls "a family to me," has continued to hire her for numerous documentaries. She has also had the chance to branch out, to work for ABC's "20/20" and NBC's "Prime Time Saturday." Beyond television, she's been an apprentice to the gifted cinematographer, Nestor Almendros, for the Academy Award-winning film, *Kramer versus Kramer*. Again, during the summer of 1980, she was an apprentice camerawoman for Peter Bogdanovich's *They All Laughed*. During the shooting of this film, she went a step beyond her apprenticeship role in *Kramer versus Kramer*. For several days during the filming she was the feature operator—the first woman ever to be given that much responsibility. Finally, in the two years she's been freelancing, Risa and her younger brother, Jim, have formed their own production

Risa shooting on location for the feature film, *They All Laughed*, directed by Peter Bogdanovich.

company, called "The Korrises." To this family partnership Jim Korris brings a master's degree in business from Harvard University as well as a good deal of professional experience as both a cameraman and sound man.

In her spacious five-room apartment overlooking the southern end of Central Park, Risa talks with a visitor one morning about her career. In this comfortable setting with its low-slung modern furniture upholstered entirely in an off-white shade, all the disparate threads of Risa's life converge. On the walls hang her paintings — bigger-than-life, boldly colored portraits of women that are part of a series she's doing on the varying roles of women in society. Among them is an obvious self-portrait, a woman with long brown hair, dressed in jeans and carrying a large camera. Next to it are several canvases depicting exotic Polynesian women in their native garb. In her bedroom is a videotape recorder on which all the television shows she has filmed can be recorded for later viewing. Clearly this apartment, so devoid of frill, is the home of a busy and organized woman, a woman whose artistic instincts are as much a part of her personal life as they are of her profession.

Recently Risa's five-year marriage to a lawyer ended. She insists that the break-up had nothing to do with the demands of her work, adding that her husband was very understanding about that. "It would be almost impossible to be married and have children if I were still working on daily news," she says. "But that's not true with documentaries, and it's even less true as a freelancer. Now I finally have some time I can call my own."

Indeed, since going freelance, Risa spends whatever spare time she has painting. Film and painting are closely related, she feels. On trips to museums she automatically notes the framing, composition, and lighting in paintings because these qualities are so similar in film. It works the other way around, too. "I was finding that my paintings were missing a lot of light that I was getting in film. When I applied the lighting techniques of film to my paintings, I could really see the difference."

While Risa talks the phone interrupts continuously. When she's not out filming, these phone calls are always a part of her mornings. It might be a TV producer, asking if she can put together a crew for a new documentary. Or another might be from a member of her crew asking some technical question. In addition to her painting and

Risa turns her camera on Olympics hero Bruce Jenner for a segment to be shown on ABC's "20/20."

filming, it is obvious that as cohead of a brand-new production company, Risa has also become something of an executive.

She credits her years on staff at CBS for enabling her to make a living as a freelance. "Nothing counts like experience. For five years I shot every single day of my life. Few cameramen can say the same; freelancers may not work for weeks. But I can shoot in my sleep. It's like falling off a log."

Being a good cameraman, according to Risa, involves far more than knowing how to operate a camera. The editing, lighting, and sound techniques she's learned have been essential, particularly now that she's become more involved with overall production. She is glad, too, for the training she had in videotape, which she still uses when the situation calls for it. But, she adds, "I feel that my greatest ability is organizing a shoot. If you could just go and do the shooting, that would be easy. But something is bound to go wrong—it always does. Some days the car breaks down or the airport traffic is snarled or you misplace a piece of equipment, and you're thrown off schedule. You have to teach yourself never to get flustered, because that's not going to help."

Risa has never felt that her sex was a disadvantage among the people she's worked with most closely. Never, in all the years she's

Risa takes a light reading of actress Nancy Walker, the director of The Village People's "Can't Stop The Music," to be featured on ABC's "20/20."

been filming, have the men in her crews treated her in a manner that could be construed as patronizing or condescending. Even when she first joined her predominantly male union, she was treated as an equal. By 1980 she was sitting on the executive board of the union.

She feels strongly, however, that a camerawoman has more difficulty being hired for certain jobs than a cameraman. Moreover, when she first joined the documentary staff at CBS, she was constantly being assigned what were referred to as "women's subjects"—stories on childbirth or homosexuality or raising children. "Being a woman yourself, you will understand this story," producers would say. And they continue saying it to her to this day.

Risa bristles when she talks about this subtle but nonetheless insidious form of discrimination. "The fact is that as a woman I'm probably less equipped to do a film on childbirth. I'm *too* empathetic! It's more upsetting for me than for a man. On the other hand, I just finished shooting a story about a new tank the army has developed. It was great. We risked life and limb and you couldn't have told what sex I was."

One instance of sexism was particularly annoying. A woman producer hired Risa's former assistant, a man with far less experience and qualifications than she, simply because the filming was to take place inside a federal prison for men. The producer explained that she had to hire a man because of the convicts and the setting. "That's ridiculous," says Risa. "If somebody wants his face on film, he's not going to care who is taking the picture. But in dangerous situations some producers look to the crew to protect them. They want the cameraman to be a big, beefy guy." She laughs. "Well, I'm not worried about my own safety, but I'm not sure I could pull out a Colt 45 and protect the producer."

She continues. "In documentaries, I feel I'm always having to fight the fact that they don't think I'm rugged enough. I have to do things more dangerously, risk more in order to convince them not to worry."

Exactly how far is she willing to go to prove herself? "Well," she says, "what you have to ask yourself is whether you're willing to go into a war zone. Do you want to take the risk of dying? But that's a question that both men and women have to ask. I was approached about going into Cambodia. I decided against it. Later, though, I said yes for a film to be shot in Zimbabwe, but the project was cancelled."

As Risa looks ahead, it is clear that fear for her own safety would never prevent her from doing a film that intrigued her. She is full of goals for the future. She wants more and more to do with producing film. She also wants to work on more hour-long television documentaries where it's possible to have time to really build a story. "If I could do anything I wanted," she adds, "I would be working on a feature, either for television or the movies, or I'd be shooting commercials." In her eyes there is little difference between a commercial for, let's say, Burger King and a full-length feature film. Both are shot in thirty-five millimeter; both require the same large crews. And because both have the highest production value and are the most costly of any kind of film, these are the two areas where there has been the most rigid resistance to including women on crews.

Thus, for Risa, the goal of becoming a cinematographer, the prestigious title given to those who are fully in charge of all filming on a feature film, continues to elude her. If and when it ever happens — and she is frankly discouraged about the prospects — that will be a real breakthrough for women. Meanwhile she refuses to put aside the goal. "I really love shooting film so much. And if you love what you're doing, you want to get more advanced in it. I'll always want to go on and get to the next step."

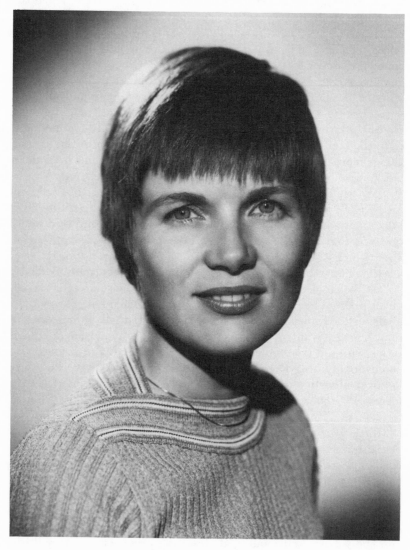

Judy Wormington, Promotion Manager for CBS affiliate relations.

CHAPTER 7

JUDY WORMINGTON

□ PROMOTION MANAGER □

JUDY WORMINGTON TYPIFIES most people who have careers in television. Although she's worked in the industry all of her adult life, she's never once had her face on the screen. Nor has she ever been sent off on an assignment to some exotic, far-off place. She has never written, researched, or in any way helped produce a single television show. And she is as amazed as anyone when she hears about the million dollar contracts awarded to the stars of her industry.

"I live on the edge of the glamour,"says Judy, describing her job. That may be true, but in many respects Judy *is* the television industry. As a promotion manager for CBS's affiliate relations, she is among thousands of people who work in various jobs on the business side of television. And that's what television is all about. First and last, it is a business — and a very profitable one at that. It depends on people like Judy to keep it that way.

Profits in commercial television relate directly to the popularity of programs. The larger the audience the bigger the profits. The networks gauge the size of their audiences by subscribing to outside, impartial rating services, the most powerful and influential of which are the ratings of the A.C. Nielsen Company. If the Nielsen ratings show, for instance, that the CBS program that is on from eight to nine o'clock Tuesday nights draws a greater percentage of viewers than the ABC or NBC programs at the same time, then CBS will be able to charge its advertisers more than its rival networks.

One way the networks assure themselves of large audiences is by signing contracts with local stations throughout the country in which they agree to pay the stations to carry primarily their programming.

When a local station signs a contract with CBS, it then becomes a CBS affiliate and generally cannot carry the programs of the other two networks. But all the networks know that their affiliate relationships are not necessarily permanent ones. If a network can keep its programs high on the Nielsen ratings chart, then their affiliates will be happy. But if their programs fall in popularity, then a local station may switch its affiliation to one of the other networks.

And that's where Judy comes in. Her job, and the job of more than forty other people who work with her in CBS's headquarters in New York, is to keep the affiliates happy. Once the network's programming has been set for the coming season, always several months before the new season begins, Judy and her group take it to the affiliates. First they must convince these local stations that the new programming will be a tremendous hit with viewers. Then, having hopefully filled the affiliates with enthusiasm, they will go on to promote the programs to viewers across the country.

Judy is ideally suited for her job. She is not simply a woman sitting in some corporate office in New York analyzing figures and decreeing what all the people west of the Hudson River will want to see on television. Judy is not from New York. She was born in Thermopolis, Wyoming; grew up in Garden City, Missouri; and has spent most of her television career working at local stations hundreds of miles west of New York City. No one has to tell her about the concerns and tastes of local viewers.

When Judy talks about her early years in Wyoming, she can't resist smiling when the New Yorker who listens to her has instant visions of cowboys and cattle branding and riding the range. It wasn't that way at all, she says. Born in 1941, she lived with her family at the edge of Thermopolis, a town of about two thousand people. Life there was no different from life in any small town. Her father was a construction worker and her mother a former beautician. When Judy was six, the family moved to the rural community of Garden City, Missouri.

By the age of eleven Judy had decided that someday she wanted to be a newspaper reporter. "I liked writing and I loved the idea of traveling and talking to people in all walks of life," she explains. She particularly envied her aunt who got to travel all over the United States and Europe working as a personal secretary for the popular singer Frances Langford. Judy had gone on trips out west to visit relatives, but she'd never been east of the Mississippi River.

All through high school she continued dreaming of being a newspaper reporter. In 1959 she entered the School of Journalism at the University of Missouri. Like everyone else in that program, she knew she would be spending her first two years taking a range of liberal arts courses before going on to specialize in journalism. But in the middle of her sophomore year, she began realizing that there were other areas for would-be journalists besides newspapers. A close friend in the School of Journalism had chosen to specialize in broadcasting. Her friend loved what she was doing so much that Judy decided she'd try broadcasting, too. "I've never had any reason to regret that decision," she adds.

The University of Missouri provided unusually good vocational training for television broadcasting. In class, students were taught something about every area of television — news reporting, production, and film-making as well as the business techniques involved in promotion and sales. Even though Judy wasn't particularly interested in production, she learned how to edit film and how to operate the huge TV cameras used at that time. In preparation for a career as a television journalist, she was taught how to write news assignments in on-air television prose, using simple, direct language and short sentences or phrases instead of the long sentences and more complicated language of print journalists.

Complementing the classroom work was the required lab work, which in this case consisted of a fully operating commercial television station where students could put what they'd learned to use. With teachers from the university supervising, students filled the position of on-air reporters, cameramen, anchors, directors, floor managers, editors, and producers. The station had no outside employees. Students also promoted the station's programs to the community and sold commercial time to advertisers. "It was the best experience I could have had," says Judy. "When I graduated in 1963, I didn't have to be trained. I was ready to go to work."

But in terms of women, the real world of broadcasting operated under a somewhat different set of rules from the cloistered world at college. Following graduation, Judy was married to a young man she'd known at the university. Together, they set out for Kansas City, Missouri's largest city and the one with the most broadcasting facilities. But she soon discovered that there was no room for her in either radio or television journalism. All the news positions, both on camera and off, were filled. No one exactly told her that they wouldn't hire her because she was a woman, but they didn't have to spell it out. As she could easily see, news jobs were men's jobs. Apparently the broadcasting industry intended to keep it that way.

Other doors in broadcasting were not so tightly closed to women. People were impressed by the thorough training of graduates of the University of Missouri. When a job in program promotion opened up at KMBC-TV, Judy was offered the position. "I realized that the only job I could have gotten in news was as a secretary," says Judy. "I didn't want that. I decided that if I went into promotion I'd have more independence and much more fun."

Although her new job put her squarely on the business side of television, there was much that was creative about the work. In charge of on-air program promotion, she designed, wrote, and produced the film strips that promoted future programs to viewers. Because KMBC at that time was both a television station and an AM-FM radio station housed under one roof, she worked closely with the radio disc jockeys in selecting background music for her on-air spots. Additionally, she handled all press relations for the station, inviting reviewers from local newspapers to advance screenings of new shows and announcing personnel changes that took place at the station.

"It's much more fun working for a local station than it is at the network level," says Judy. "At KMBC I had freedom to move about and see what was going on in every area. I suppose there were nearly 150 of us at the station, but we were like a big family. You never have that feeling of closeness when you work for the networks."

Being at a local station, adds Judy, is the best way to understand how the television industry works. For the television industry is not the giant networks located in New York but the hundreds and hundreds of local stations all over the country. Among these stations, some are owned and operated by the networks, others are network affiliates, and still others are independent stations with no affiliations. In the past, Very High Frequency stations (or VHFs) produced a far clearer picture on television screens than stations operating on Ultra High Frequency (UHF) transmissions. Therefore, VHF stations were considered far more valuable.

Anyone can own a television station. But nobody or no one group is allowed to own more than seven — five VHF stations and two UHF stations. The networks are permitted to own only five VHF stations, all of which are located in the nation's largest cities. Though the networks and local stations are privately owned, the air waves that they use for their broadcasts are owned by the public. In return for the use of these air waves, the networks and local stations are licensed by the federal government and must pledge that a portion of their programs will serve the public interest. In the case of the networks, this means that a certain amount of programming must be devoted to news and national affairs. In like manner, local stations must be able to prove that a good portion of their programs reflects the station's involvement with the special concerns and problems of their own communities. If they disregard this pledge, they know that the Federal Communications Commission (F.C.C.) can take away their license to broadcast.

Occupying the top position at local stations is the station manager. This is the person who carries overall responsibility for the way the station is run. It is he (and in almost all cases it's traditionally been a man) who reports to the owners, keeps tabs on the profits and losses, and is in charge of maintaining good community relations.

There are usually three people who are in positions of equal importance under the station manager. One is the programming director; the other is the sales manager; the third is the business manager.

The programming director plans the station's program schedule and keeps up to date with whether or not each program is popular with local viewers. Stations like KMBC-TV in Kansas City, which are network affiliates, have neither the money nor the access to talent that it takes to produce their own entertainment shows. Therefore, most of their programs are network shows. With few exceptions, local stations produce only local news, local interviews and public affairs programs, and local sports events. In her job in program promotion at KMBC, Judy reported directly to the programming director.

The sales manager at local stations oversees the selling of commercial time to advertisers and is responsible for knowing, if sales are down, why they are down. Working directly under the sales manager are the national sales manager, who oversees sales to national advertisers; the local sales manager, who sells to local advertisers; and the general sales manager, who coordinates all sales.

Working for the national sales manager is a sales representative, usually referred to as a "sales rep." The sales rep is not located at the station but works out of such cities as New York, Los Angeles, Chicago, Atlanta, and Dallas. In these cities are the large advertising agencies that represent big national companies. When these companies have products that will sell only in a few regional markets, they would much rather buy commercial space directly from the local stations in these markets than go to the expense of advertising through the networks. But local stations must have someone to represent them to these potential advertisers. That's why they hire sales reps from the cities.

Although people who work on the business side of television do a variety of things — sales, programming, community relations, promotion — the goal is the same. Basically they are in the business of having programs that will attract advertising dollars and make profits for the station. As a profit-making business, there is little room for idealism. Critics can rant and rave all they want about the poor quality of programs, but if these programs are popular with viewers, they will also be popular with advertisers and stations. That being the case, there is little chance that they will be replaced by programs of better quality.

Judy continued doing promotion for KMBC for six years. In 1969 the station's promotion director, her boss, left to become the station manager in Dayton, Ohio. With his job vacant, Judy was called into the station manager's office and asked whether she wanted it. Immediately she said yes. But a few days later it was publicly announced that a young woman who'd been working as the station's artist, a woman with no experience in promotion whatsoever, had been made the new director of promotion. Judy was hurt and she was furious. She and everyone else at the station knew about the "special relationship" between the station manager and the woman who had been selected.

"You see a lot of that kind of thing in television, or at least you do in the areas I've worked," says Judy. "I guess it was probably worse in the 1960's than it is now, but I've known a lot of women who have felt that the only way they could get ahead professionally was by getting romantically involved with some man in the business."

Judy was so angry at what had happened that it became untenable to remain at the station. Quitting her job, she followed her former boss to Dayton. But soon she decided that she really wasn't nearly as happy in Ohio as she thought she might be. Returning home, she was rehired at KMBC, this time as assistant to the station's programming director.

Now her primary responsibility was as a liaison between the station and community groups. In television parlance, this function is called "ascertainment" and involves the station's pledge to the F.C.C. to ascertain what the concerns and problems of the community are in order to focus on them in local programs. Not only was Judy the one who set up regular meetings with community groups, but because of her close contacts with these groups, she was involved also in the process of filing for the three-year renewal of the station's license. In addition she handled calls to the station from local viewers. "Mostly these came in when our regular programming was interrupted," Judy explains. "When a soap opera like "General Hospital" was replaced by a special event like the moon shot, our switchboard was jammed with calls from furious viewers."

She goes on. "But this strong community involvement is another reason I found working for a local television station so satisfying. You get involved with community problems because you care, because it's your community. And you get involved because you have to, because that's part of the station's pledge to the F.C.C. It's entirely different when you work at the network level. You're just too removed from local problems to feel much involvement."

One year after returning to KMBC, Judy moved over into radio, becoming the promotion manager for one of the local stations. She had been there nearly a year when the general manager called her into his office to tell her that the program director had decided that he'd rather do all his own promotion. In short she was fired. Before long she had another job, this one as assistant to the program manager of a new Ultra High Frequency independent station in Kansas City. But that station soon went bankrupt, or as Judy says, "went dark," and she was out of a job again. Almost immediately she was hired as assistant to the program director at KCMO-TV, the CBS affiliate in Kansas City.

In little over three years, Judy had had five broadcasting jobs. In other industries this might be viewed as a sign of incompetence or instability. Not so in television. For one thing, all of Judy's jobs were

"I live on the edge of the glamour," says Judy of her behind-the-scenes job in the business end of the enormously profitable television industry.

middle-level jobs rather than managerial positions. In the fast-paced, always changing business of television, people get hired and fired with the same rapidity as programs are introduced and fade. The vast majority of television people harbor no great burning loyalty to the stations they happen to be working for at any given moment. What's important are their own careers within the broadcasting industry at large.

By 1972 Judy's private life had become far more important to her than her television life. After years of being single, she had fallen in love and was planning to be married. Both she and her fiancé had been married before. When Judy was straight out of college, she had been in a marriage that ended in divorce after only three years. This time, however, she felt the situation was different. Not only was she older and more mature, but she and her husband-to-be, Bill Wormington, had much in common. He had been working in television since the late 1940's, just about the time of its birth. Recently he had become national sales manager for an independent station in Kansas City. Because his job required his being in New York City much of the time, he and Judy decided to move there.

Once again during the next few years Judy switched jobs frequently. She began by working part time for H.R. Television, a sales rep firm that put local stations in contact with national advertisers. Two years later, feeling more settled in New York and wanting to resume a full-time career, she took a job at the Television Bureau of Advertising. Here she expanded her background in research, becoming more involved in analyzing Nielsen figures and working on sales promotions. With this new expertise she then became the new promotion manager for the New York radio station WNEW. Finally in late 1978 she became manager of promotion for the affiliate relations department at CBS.

Judy came to CBS just as the network was in the process of redesigning its affiliate relations department. From the beginning days of television in the late 1940's, CBS always was the number-one network. It outdistanced its competitors not only in overall ratings but also in the size of its empire of affiliates. Since local stations were delighted to be associated with the network that ran the most popular programs on the air, CBS didn't have to spend much time convincing them to remain affiliates. Suddenly in the late 1970's the situation began to change, CBS was running neck and neck with NBC and, worse, there seemed a danger that ABC, traditionally in last place, would overtake everyone. Quickly CBS revamped its affiliate relations department, putting more emphasis on research services and on actually getting out there and courting the affiliates. To do this, they added ten more people. Among these ten were Judy and four other women — the first women to be hired in the department's history.

In working for CBS Judy has gone full circle in television. Having come from local stations that were being serviced by the networks, she is now at a network doing the servicing. In her present job she uses everything she's learned in the past. To promote CBS's new programs, she often produces her own video cassettes. But she says, "What I mainly do now is work on presentations and ratings information for the affiliates."

Sometimes she remembers her old goal of becoming a television journalist and wishes rather wistfully that she had more contact with the excitement and glamour in the creative end of the industry where news, documentaries, and entertainment are actually being produced. But then again she says there are compensations to being on the business end. Business people are generally paid better than those on the creative side. Also, producers, directors, and news people are usually required to work long, unpredictable hours. Judy values her nine-to-five working day, which leaves her plenty of time to be with her husband, see friends, attend weekly yoga classes, and spend several hours each week jogging in Central Park.

Besides, she insists, her job is not without some aspects of the excitement and glamour that exist elsewhere in the industry. It's fun to be behind the scenes, knowing about the network's new programs before anyone else. Since her department is the one that announces each season's schedule to the press and to the affiliates, she must preview every new show in order to know what she's promoting. Then with the announcement of the new season's schedule, she is off for a week-long meeting with officials from the affiliate stations, usually held in some city other than New York. Here the programs are unveiled with appropriate hullabaloo, including appearances by most of the glamorous show people who will be stars of the new season.

The meeting held in Los Angeles in the spring of 1980 was a particularly festive occasion, says Judy. There it was announced that CBS had won the 1979–1980 ratings race, edging out ABC by 0.1

of a ratings point. To most people that may seem an infinitessimal figure, but not to people like Judy. An 0.1 average over a thirty-one-week season means that CBS reached 192 million viewers more than ABC, its nearest competitor.

All in all Judy sees her life in television these days as having a nice kind of wholeness. Her past and present experiences have merged, creating a career that is both satisfying and sensible. In speaking of the future, she says, "I'd like to go back to work at a local station because that's where the fun is. Then again, there are so many things happening in the industry that have exciting implications for the future. Satellite communications is one. Now, there's an area I'd like to get into!"

Clearly Judy is a television person. In speaking about herself, where she's been, and where she's going, she can't avoid talking about television. Television is her past, her present, and her future.

Chloe Aaron, Senior Vice-president for Programming at PBS. *(Photo Courtesy PBS)*

CHAPTER 8

CHLOE AARON

□ SENIOR VICE-PRESIDENT FOR PROGRAMMING □

CHLOE WELLINGHAM AARON is that rare exception in television—a woman at the top. In 1976 she was named Senior Vice-president for Programming at the Public Broadcasting Service. Not only was she the first woman ever to have attained a vice-presidency in that organization, but the press release announcing her appointment said she was "believed to be the highest-ranking woman at the network level in the history of television."

"Compared to *what?*" was Chloe's irreverent response. To her the honor was a dubious one, significant more because women were (and still are) so underrepresented in the power circles of network television than because of her own distinction.

Yet Chloe does not underrate the importance of her job. As head of programming, she has the power to decide what millions of Americans will see on television. The Public Broadcasting Service, often referred to simply as PBS, is charged with developing and distributing a national schedule of programs for public television stations across the country. At PBS Chloe is the senior person responsible for selecting these programs. Nothing that carries the PBS name on it and is seen on public TV during the prime-time evening hours is there without her approval.

What qualified her for such a powerful position? That's what a group of college students wanted to know when they invited her to speak to them on the topic, "How to Get a Job in Broadcasting." At the time she was new in her job. But she knew perfectly well what the students wanted to hear—a neat little step-by-step formula, based on her own experience, for getting ahead in television. That's what worried her. She had no formula, no tried-and-true tidbits of advice. Finally, at the very last minute, she decided to tell the truth.

"I bet you assume that I started my television career by getting my B.A. in Communications," she said as an opener.

Out in the audience heads bobbed up and down.

"And then you probably think I went on and got my master's degree in Communications at Columbia University."

Again all heads nodded.

"Then probably you think I started at the bottom at some local station and worked my way up."

The students kept nodding. This was the standard way of going into broadcasting and they knew it.

"Well," said Chloe, "that's not the way it was at all. Until I got my present job at PBS, the idea of working in television never even occurred to me."

The audience had come to hear a formula. What they got was one woman's story. They learned that Chloe had once had specific career ambitions, but that in the process of growing and responding to whatever challenges had come along and interested her at the time, she had deviated from her original course. One working experience had led to another with each building from the one before. Finally, to her own surprise, she had found herself in television. What's more, she had arrived at the top.

And so, in concluding her speech, Chloe added, "If you want to be successful in broadcasting, my advice is to do something substantive first. Try to carve out an area of responsibility for yourself. Because as far as I can see, this pyramid structure of trying to work yourself up from the bottom to the top doesn't work. Most organizations, television included, bring people in from the outside to fill the top jobs."

Probably the best reason that Chloe never considered having a career in television is that she grew up without it. Born in Los Angeles in 1938, she was the only child of parents who had some doubts about the wisdom of owning the new machine. Long after their neighbors had acquired sets, Mr. and Mrs. Wellingham kept holding out. They finally broke down and got one when Chloe was eighteen.

As a little girl growing up in southern California, Chloe never felt that she would end up being only a wife and a mother. That seemed much too boring. She was a very good student, both at high school in Arcadia, California, and later at Occidental College. Above all she loved to write and she was equally drawn to anything that had to do with the theater. Wondering how she could combine these two main interests into some kind of future career, she finally hit upon what seemed the perfect solution. She would become a drama critic, writing reviews about the theater.

With this goal in mind, she continued her studies. An English major at Occidental College, she spent much of her spare time writing for the campus literary review and doing freelance newspaper articles for *The Pasadena Star News*. After receiving her B.A. in 1960 she took a job as a researcher at the Huntington Library where she worked as an assistant to the famous historian Alan Nevins. "That was terrific," she says. "I did a lot of work for him on such things as Civil War diaries."

In 1961 Chloe moved to Washington, D.C. Immediately she embarked on a master's program in American Literary Cultural History at George Washington University. She still wanted to be a drama critic, but she felt that this additional education could only enrich her background for that. One year later she was married to David Aaron, a man she'd known since her senior year in college. By now he was in the U.S. Foreign Service and also living in Washington — at least temporarily. Shortly after he and Chloe were married, he was assigned to go to Ecuador. As his wife, Chloe was allowed to go along.

Marriage to a man in the Foreign Service may sound like an interesting and glamorous life, but most wives report otherwise. Constantly following their husbands around from one foreign post to the next, they never live anywhere long enough to become part of a community or to develop their own interests within it. Usually not speaking the language and unfamiliar with the native customs, they remain outsiders. They live in American communities, stick closely to American friends, and while away the time with other Foreign Service wives reminiscing about the way things are back home.

Chloe was not the typical Foreign Service wife by any means. "When we got to Ecuador," she says, "I saw that there was no chance to be a drama critic because there was no live theater. So," she adds matter-of-factly, "I did the obvious thing. I started a theater. I was twenty-three years old, just out of school, and it seemed very important to get busy quickly."

Chloe ran her theater the entire two years the Aarons were in Ecuador. Productions were staged both in English and in Spanish. Not only did she find people to design sets and costumes, but she conducted all casting in both languages. This gave her a whole life in the Spanish community that she ordinarily would not have had. "The theater did very well," she says with pride. "We made lots of money and we donated it to a local orphanage."

Chloe and David returned to Washington in 1964. Before leaving for Ecuador, Chloe had completed all of her requirements for her master's degree except for writing her thesis. Now she did that. In addition, she took a job as editor for *The National Banking Review*. Recalling that period in her life, she smiles. "I was all over the place in those years. I went from having run a theater in Spanish to editing articles written by economists and reworking them into language that the ordinary reader could understand."

Throughout the 1960's, she also wrote a great deal on her own. When she and David moved with the Foreign Service to Paris for a year, she continued writing in France. They came back to Washington and she gave birth to their son, Timothy. She kept writing — and, what's more, selling her articles with increasing frequency. By the end of the 1960's, she had become a full-time freelance journalist, with articles appearing regularly in such publications as *The Washington Post, The Washington Star, Art in America,* and *New York Magazine*. She wrote about what she cared about, with one slight difference: "I found when I started freelancing that I was writing more and more about film and television than I was about drama."

Television, particularly alternative television, was a very topical subject in the late 1960's. Ten years earlier, alternative television had meant educational television, in the strictest sense. But that hadn't given the public much of an alternative. In 1959 only forty-four educational stations were on the air and most of those broadcast only a few hours a day. Typical programs often consisted of one teacher spouting forth math or science or Spanish lessons into a camera. It wasn't the kind of programming, certainly, that attracted a wide audience or offered much of an alternative to what the commercial networks were broadcasting.

The 1960's changed forever the focus of noncommercial television. In 1962 NET (National Educational Television) became a New
York-based producing unit. Supported by the Ford Foundation, it
began supplying the educational stations with national programs,
particularly documentaries and public affairs shows. Because the
educational stations could not afford the elaborate interconnection
facilities used by the commercial networks and their affiliates, NET
had to mail tapes of its programs to the stations. Whenever the mails
arrived with new tapes, the stations would broadcast them. It was a
primitive system of distribution, but a start. It made everyone realize
that noncommercial television could be vastly improved with a system of national programming.

In 1967 the United States Congress passed the Public Broadcasting Act. This provided annual federal funds for the development
and distribution of national programs by satellite to the nation's
noncommercial stations. At this point noncommercial television lost
its old name of educational television and became known as it is
today, public television.

And what is public television, other than independent,
advertising-free broadcasting? In the report of the Carnegie Commission on Educational Television, which was one of the studies that
led to the Public Broadcasting Act, it was defined this way: "We seek
freedom from the constraints . . . of commercial television. We seek
. . . freedom from the pressures of inadequate funds. We seek for the
artist, the technician, the scholar, and the public servant freedom to
create, freedom to innovate, freedom to be heard in this most far-
reaching medium. We seek for the citizen freedom to view, to see
programs that the present system, by its incompleteness, denies
him." In short, the goal was that public television would offer at last a
real alternative to viewers.

Intrigued by what was going on within the alternate television
movement, Chloe wrote an article about it. In it she mentioned the
possibility of public TV becoming a place where wonderful new films
could be shown that might otherwise never reach the American
public. When it was published, Washington's National Endowment
for the Arts contacted her, asking her to explore ways it could give
away money effectively to film, television, and radio. As its consultant, Chloe spent months traveling all over the country. Everywhere
she went she talked to independent film producers as well as to radio
and television station managers, trying to ascertain their basic needs

as well as their dreams. After completing her study and writing up a report, the National Endowment for the Arts asked her to become a permanent member of its staff, starting up the program she had suggested and implementing it.

Chloe was the director of the National Endowment's Public Media Program for the next six years. This position put her in charge of all of its activities that related to the funding of film, television, and radio. It also put her in the position of being an active participant in the embryonic period of public television.

After the Public Broadcasting Act had passed, the Corporation for Public Broadcasting was established to administer the new federal funds. This organization, however, was prohibited by law from operating as a network with a planned, nationwide schedule of programs. Thus PBS was founded, a Washington-based organization that was to operate the satellite-connected system and develop programs for national distribution. By 1971 some of the facilities that connected PBS to the nation's public TV stations were still being built.

But, partly due to Chloe's efforts, PBS began immediately to develop some very fine programs. The National Endowment for the Arts was responsible for funding such major PBS productions as "Dance in America" as well as a series of symphony orchestra concerts called "Live From Lincoln Center." Perhaps the most innovative project that Chloe helped to get on public television was "Vision," an original American drama series. Under her leadership, the National Endowment joined with the Ford Foundation and agreed to try to get good, contemporary drama on the air, plays written by relatively unknown American writers who had never had their works seen on television before. These days Chloe has mixed feelings about this last criteria. Although the "Vision" series gave tremendous encouragement to many unknown writers, the productions on a whole were uneven. Says Chloe, "If I had to do it all over again, I wouldn't limit it to people who had never written for TV before."

In 1976 Chloe was asked to join the Public Broadcasting Service as head of programming. In this position, the only person superior to her was the president. And yet, in spite of having never worked directly in television before, no one questioned her knowledge of the medium. Nor did anyone have doubts about her qualifications for the job. She had already proved herself elsewhere.

In the headquarters of PBS in Washington D.C., Chloe keeps close tabs on all prime-time PBS-distributed programs shown by public television stations all over the country. *(Photo Courtesy PBS)*

Still, she says, "There was so much I had to learn when I first got there, and I knew it. I thought I had a good background for developing shows and writing about them through the funding I'd done at the National Endowment for the Arts. But then again, I knew that program scheduling and commissioning new shows was going to be a whole new aspect."

Having already been in a top executive position, she knew that she must immediately build her own staff. This meant lots of firing and lots of hiring. In terms of women, she had found that PBS was as bad as the networks. Except for her, there were no women in any positions of responsibility. From the start she established the hiring of women and minority group members as a "professional goal." Public television, she felt strongly, had a responsibility to reflect the country's rich diversity of cultures and points of view not only on the air, but behind the scenes as well. Today, because of her efforts and those of the president of PBS, Lawrence Grossman, women are *fully* represented on every level at PBS.

Chloe faced another big problem when she first came to PBS. The relationship between PBS and the country's public television stations was not as good as it should have been. What was missing was trust. The local stations had always cherished their independence and stressed the importance of their own local programming. They were terrified that PBS would start acting and behaving like a fourth network, telling them how to run things back home.

PBS is a voluntary membership organization. More than 150 stations, or roughly three-fifths of all public TV stations in the country, belong to it. These member-stations each pay a certain yearly amount to PBS, which accounts for about one-fifth of PBS's total budget. In return, the stations get a nationally developed schedule of programs as well as other support services. Member-stations have the right to decide for themselves which PBS programs to carry and which not to carry. When Chloe first came to PBS, the stations were also insisting that it was their right to broadcast PBS programs whenever they saw fit. This meant that one station might broadcast a PBS program on one night while another station might not run the same program until a week later.

Television viewers are creatures of habit. They want to know that a favorite program can be seen on a regular, predictable schedule whether they happen to be in Dallas or Chicago. What's more, if a viewer knows that his favorite program can be seen every Wednesday night, then he is very apt to stay with the same channel the rest of the evening. The commercial networks have always known this; public television, fearful of becoming too much like the networks, was reluctant to acknowledge it.

"I had been at PBS for about two years before we began to trust each other," Chloe says. Finally she was able to persuade the member-stations to experiment with a scheme for partial national program scheduling. Under this plan, called Common Carriage, the stations agreed to broadcast the very best PBS programs at the same time throughout the country from Sunday through Wednesday night. With its programs being shown simultaneously everywhere, it was then possible for PBS to promote these programs in such national publications as *TV Guide*. "And it worked," adds Chloe. "Since we've had some national promotion of our programs, our audiences have increased 25 percent." She counts this as her greatest accomplishment since coming to PBS.

PBS does not produce any of its own programs. There are no production facilities in its Washington headquarters. If Chloe and her staff decide, for example, that PBS should bring a good comedy

Chloe sees public television as the only place where viewers can find programs that offer an exciting alternative to what is being shown by the commercial networks. *(Photo Courtesy of PBS)*

series to its viewers, they will commission one of the production centers located at a variety of public television stations to produce the series. The largest number of PBS productions comes from New York's NET, which in 1971 was merged into that city's public television station. Boston and Los Angeles also produce a good deal of PBS programming. But other public stations also contribute. During the 1977–1978 season, fifty-three stations produced programs that were distributed by PBS.

Another big source for PBS programs, particularly documentaries, comes from independent producers. Generally, an independently produced program will come to PBS through an individual station, which arranges to acquire it on behalf of the system.

A third source comes from overseas, primarily from Great Britain. Imported programs, however, are somewhat of a sensitive subject at PBS. During the 1979–1980 season, PBS staffers were pleased to report that they had only one British import, "Masterpiece Theatre." The feeling is that since PBS is part of American public television, it should feature American productions. But original productions are costly, often more than $300,000 for an hour of viewing, whereas foreign productions can be bought for one-tenth of that figure. "Recently," reports Chloe, "there has been a turnabout. Instead of us buying from the British, they are buying more and more from us."

Certainly one of the reasons for British interest is that American public television has been improving. Some of its programs have finally gotten enough funding so that they could be produced properly with no shortcuts. At home, audiences have increased not only because the programs are better and have begun being promoted on a national scale, but also because they are presented more professionally. "In some cases," says Chloe, "the local stations have been leaders in making public television better. The Chicago station, for instance, has always been very successful in terms of attracting a large audience. The transition between their programs was crisp; they always had good promotion for shows later in the evening. They were so good, in fact, that we took them as a model for other stations."

Like the commercial networks, PBS subscribes to the Nielsen ratings. In the early days of public television, when idealism was rampant, this adherence to ratings might have seemed at odds with the whole concept of public television. The idea then was that public TV would be able to present quality programming because, unlike the networks, it alone would be free of advertisers, free of having to make a profit, and free of the necessity to compete for viewers.

These days, there is still a good deal of idealism, but this is tempered by a very real awareness that public television is a business. Quite simply, it is in the business of presenting programs that will be properly funded and will attract viewers. "The ratings matter a lot to me," says Chloe. "We are not going to present sitcoms just so we can get high ratings, but we do care about the size of our audience."

In prime time the average PBS-distributed program is watched by about 1.5 million families. This figure may seem large but it is really very small when compared to the number of viewers tuning in to the commercial networks. According to one PBS staffer, "Our highest-rated show had a national rating of 15, and in commercial TV a show with that kind of rating would be taken off the air." Nonetheless, in scheduling PBS programs, Chloe looks closely at what is being offered during the same time slots by the commercial networks. And from time to time she allows herself to talk about a "developing competition." Clearly she would love to give the big three networks a run for their money.

The competition might be more equitable if PBS had the same kind of budget as the networks. In 1979 PBS had $80,000,000 — more money than it had ever had in its history. Yet this was peanuts compared to the $700,000,000 spent by each of the commercial networks. "Money is *always* a problem," says Chloe. "It takes us about eighteen months to get a good series off the ground. The only times we don't have to worry too much is for our special events coverage — instant news events like the Three Mile Island incident — for which we have a sizable yearly fund. Also we've been given $3,000,000 a year to develop programs for fund-raising during our Festival Week."

Once a year, all over the country, public television holds it Festival Week. At that time it presents its best face to the nation with its finest programs broadcast one right after the other. These are interspersed with celebrities who then pitch viewers for money to help keep public television alive. This fund-raising effort brings in roughly $10,000,000. The rest of the money comes to PBS in bits and pieces. Some comes from government organizations, some from

Chloe Aaron's original goal of becoming a drama critic has been greatly expanded. These days she is bringing theater to millions free of charge. *(Photo Courtesy PBS)*

member-stations, some from the Corporation for Public Broadcasting, and some from private foundation grants. A final way PBS raises money is through corporate underwriting. Frequently some very large and very rich corporation will decide to fund some particular PBS production rather than to advertise on commercial television. The theory is that no one loses. The public gets a first-rate program that otherwise might not be broadcast; the corporation trades off advertising revenues for an improved public image.

Public affairs programs have always proven popular with public television viewers. Year after year, the faithful keep coming back to "Wall Street Week," "The MacNeil/Lehrer Report," "Washington Week in Review," and "Bill Moyers' Journal." Why? Because this type of in-depth analysis of what's going on in the world can't be seen on commercial TV. PBS science programs like the "National Geographic" series also do well for the same reason. People can't get them anywhere else. One such show, "Einstein's Universe" with Peter Ustinoff, was so popular in New York that it beat out the prime-time movie shown at the same time. "When you start looking at the research," says Chloe, "you realize that people are hungry for information."

Should public television duplicate programs that the commercial networks do and do well? That's always a big question at PBS, especially when it comes to covering public affairs events. But most people believe that it is the duty of public television to cover newsworthy events whether the networks do them or not. Sometimes, for budgetary reasons, PBS has had to bow out. To have covered the 1980 Republican Party Convention, for instance, would have cost PBS $3,000,000, which they decided against. Says Chloe, "My feeling is that it would have been worth it if we could have done it differently from the networks. If we'd covered it, I think we should have used all of our talent—Bill Moyers, MacNeil/Lehrer, Dick Cavett, and the Muppets."

Since Chloe doesn't have to worry about those PBS programs that are proven successes, she spends the major part of her time working on new programs. She is constantly looking for ideas, trying to fill in the gaps where she feels PBS programming could be better. Once she and her staff have decided to go ahead with some new project, she follows it through in every detail from its funding to its production, final execution, and follow-up promotion. Because many

PBS programs are made at production centers around the country, she has recently replaced her husband, David, as the number-one traveler in the Aaron family.

Shortly after she came to PBS, David Aaron was named Deputy Assistant to President Carter for National Security Affairs. Working out of the White House directly under Zbigniew Brzezinski, he has had a job as demanding and high-powered as Chloe's. When asked how she feels their son, Timothy, has fared having two parents with extremely successful, full-time careers, Chloe says, "That's not an easy answer. My hunch is that it is not a problem. If I look at the things that have hurt or upset him through the years, it wasn't the fact that we both worked. It was things that happened at school or mistakes we made in hiring housekeepers." She and her husband travel separately, so that one of them is always home. And she adds, "When we're all home together, we have this kind of sacred hour, the dinner hour, when we catch up and find out what everyone has been doing during the day."

Certainly Chloe couldn't imagine giving up her work. Nor, at this point, can she imagine going from PBS to one of the commercial networks. Future possibilities for public television are too exciting.

"My first priority," she says, "is to get a good drama series going." She talks about some of the things already under way in that area. Edith Wharton's *House of Mirth,* for instance. "I saw it in rough cut and it's gorgeous! Also, John Cheever was so pleased with the way we did his short stories that he's now writing an original play for PBS." She goes on to things that could be done: "There's a play on Broadway now, *Children of a Lesser God,* that would be a natural for us. And James Earl Jones is currently in a play in New Haven, which I saw, that would be terrific. We'd take it and adapt it for television." She continues, ticking off a list of possibilities, adding, "You see, I've been caring about drama for a long time."

Indeed. And though she may have diverged from her original ambition of becoming a drama critic, she has ended up with a greatly expanded role. Instead of evaluating existing theater, Chloe Aaron is making theater happen. For that, millions of television viewers can be thankful.

Author's Note: Chloe Aaron is no longer head of programming at PBS. Shortly before this book went to the printer, she became president of the Television Corporation of America, a brand-new company in Washington that produces and distributes programs for television.

GLOSSARY

ABC (American Broadcasting Company): the youngest of the three major commercial networks, established in 1943.

ACT (Action for Children's Television): a national nonprofit consumer group working to encourage diversity and eliminate commercial abuses from children's television.

anchor: the man or woman who hosts a program of news from inside a television studio, introducing the day's stories and the reporters who have covered them. The term originated in 1952 to describe Walter Cronkite's role at the Republican and Democratic conventions.

audimeter: a machine placed in a home with the permission of the home owner, that measures the household's daily television viewing habits, and later becomes part of the data that indicates which programs are popular with the public and which are not.

broadcasting: the systematic diffusion by radio or television of entertainment and information for simultaneous reception by a scattered audience with appropriate receiving apparatus. Sound broadcasting (radio) came into being about 1920; television broadcasting began in 1936.

CATV (cable television): a system that delivers television pictures by wire rather than over the air.

CBS (Columbia Broadcasting System): the second major commercial network to be established and, by 1929, a small rival to NBC.

coaxial cable: a special kind of AT&T cable capable of carrying the wide band width required to transmit television signals over long distances. (In 1952 the first coast-to-coast cable was completed, making possible nationwide simultaneous transmission of television pictures.)

commercials: advertising seen on television. (Production costs for a thirty-second commercial can exceed $100,000; a single presentation of that commercial on a highly-rated show will cost the advertiser more than $50,000.)

Fairness Doctrine: law requiring broadcasters to provide equal access to the airwaves for competing views on important political and social matters.

F.C.C. (Federal Communications Commission): a federal agency created in 1934 that is in charge of regulating four major communication industries—telephone, telegraph, radio, and television. The F.C.C. licenses all television stations that use the publicly owned airwaves for their broadcasts. In return the stations must prove that a certain portion of their programs serve "the public interest" by providing viewers with up-to-date news, documentaries on local and national issues, forums for airing local community concerns and information.

Iconoscope: the very first type of pickup tube, invented by V.K. Zworykin in 1923 and used in most pre-World War II television sets.

NBC (National Broadcasting Company): the first full-fledged commercial broadcasting network in the United States, formed in 1926 by the Radio Corporation of America (RCA).

A.C. Nielsen ratings: an independent, impartial rating service, subscribed to by all the major networks and the Public Broadcasting Service, that monitors the percentage of homes watching individual programs at any given time.

network affiliations: the basis of networking in which local radio and television stations agree to carry one or another of the three network's programs, thus becoming an affiliate. Of the roughly 700 commercial stations that exist in the United States, more than 600 are affiliated stations.

PBS (Public Broadcasting Service): a loosely knit network of about 265 noncommercial stations that was founded in 1967, supplanting National Educational Television.

prime time: term used to designate the most prestigious, the most visible, the most profitable time for television programming—the hours between 7 P.M. and 11 P.M.

ratings: the share of audiences watching specific programs as a percentage of all TV homes in the U.S.

satellite: a relay station in the sky that receives signals from one point on earth and relays them to another point a continent or an ocean away.

sitcom (situation comedy): a series of half-hours or hours of prime-time entertainment filled with zany and always predictable characters and situations. Called by network executives "the bedrock of a successful program schedule," the sitcom originated on radio in 1928 with "The Amos 'n Andy Show." In 1979–1980, fourteen of the top twenty television shows were sitcoms.

soaps (soap opera): daytime television melodrama presented in episodic form five days a week that puts fictional characters in "real life" situations with no permanent resolution.

syndication: syndicated programs, unlike network programs, are sold to individual stations regardless of network affiliation and are seen at various times in different sections of the country.

tube: commonly used slang for television.

UHF (Ultra High Frequency): the band of airwaves, consisting of 470 to 890 million cycles per second, over which the small independent stations do their broadcasting.

VHF (Very High Frequency): the band of airwaves, consisting of 54 to 216 million cycles per second, over which most network programs are seen.

INDEX